Getting Started with Azure OpenAI

Deploying and Managing Azure AI and Azure OpenAI Solutions

Shimon Ifrah

Apress®

Getting Started with Azure OpenAI: Deploying and Managing Azure AI and Azure OpenAI Solutions

Shimon Ifrah
Melbourne, VIC, Australia

ISBN-13 (pbk): 979-8-8688-0598-1   ISBN-13 (electronic): 979-8-8688-0599-8
https://doi.org/10.1007/979-8-8688-0599-8

Managing Director, Apress Media LLC: Welmoed Spahr
Acquisitions Editor: Smriti Srivastava
Development Editor: Laura Berendson
Editorial Assistant: Kripa Joseph

Cover designed by eStudioCalamar

Cover image designed by Freepik (www.freepik.com)

Distributed to the book trade worldwide by Springer Science+Business Media New York, 1 New York Plaza, Suite 4600, New York, NY 10004-1562, USA. Phone 1-800-SPRINGER, fax (201) 348-4505, e-mail orders-ny@springer-sbm.com, or visit www.springeronline.com. Apress Media, LLC is a California LLC and the sole member (owner) is Springer Science + Business Media Finance Inc (SSBM Finance Inc). SSBM Finance Inc is a **Delaware** corporation.

For information on translations, please e-mail booktranslations@springernature.com; for reprint, paperback, or audio rights, please e-mail bookpermissions@springernature.com.

Apress titles may be purchased in bulk for academic, corporate, or promotional use. eBook versions and licenses are also available for most titles. For more information, reference our Print and eBook Bulk Sales web page at http://www.apress.com/bulk-sales.

Any source code or other supplementary material referenced by the author in this book is available to readers on GitHub. For more detailed information, please visit https://www.apress.com/gp/services/source-code.

If disposing of this product, please recycle the paper

Table of Contents

About the Author

Shimon Ifrah is a solution architect, writer, tech blogger, and an author with over 15 years of experience in the design, management, and deployment of information technology systems, applications, and networks. In the last decade, Shimon has specialized in cloud computing and containerized applications on Microsoft Azure, Azure AI, Microsoft 365, Azure DevOps, and .NET. Shimon also holds over 20 vendor certificates from Microsoft, AWS, VMware, Oracle, and Cisco. During his career in the IT industry, he has worked for some of the world's largest managed services and technology companies, assisting them in designing and managing systems used by millions of people every day. He is based in Melbourne, Australia.

About the Technical Reviewer

 **Kasam Shaikh** is a prominent figure in India's artificial intelligence landscape, holding the distinction of being one of the country's first four Microsoft Most Valuable Professionals (MVPs) in AI. Currently serving as a senior architect, Kasam boasts an impressive track record as an author, having authored five best-selling books dedicated to Azure and AI technologies. Beyond his writing endeavors, Kasam is recognized as a Microsoft Certified Trainer (MCT) and influential tech YouTuber (@mekasamshaikh). He also leads the largest online Azure AI community, known as DearAzure | Azure INDIA, and is a globally renowned AI speaker. His commitment to knowledge sharing extends to contributions to Microsoft Learn, where he plays a pivotal role.

Within the realm of AI, Kasam is a respected subject matter expert (SME) in generative AI for the cloud, complementing his role as a senior cloud architect. He actively promotes the adoption of No Code and Azure OpenAI solutions and possesses a strong foundation in hybrid and cross-cloud practices. Kasam Shaikh's versatility and expertise make him an invaluable asset in the rapidly evolving landscape of technology, contributing significantly to the advancement of Azure and AI.

In summary, Kasam Shaikh is a multifaceted professional who excels in both technical expertise and knowledge dissemination. His contributions span writing, training, community leadership, public speaking, and architecture, establishing him as a true luminary in the world of Azure and AI. Kasam was recently recognized as the top voice in AI by LinkedIn, making him the sole exclusive Indian professional acknowledged by both Microsoft and LinkedIn for his contributions to the world of artificial intelligence!

CHAPTER 1

Introduction to Azure AI and OpenAI

Thank you for choosing this book. *Getting Started with Azure OpenAI* is my fifth book and third book about Microsoft Azure. In my previous two Azure books, I focused on Microsoft Azure container services (AKS, ACR, Docker, etc.) and how to use infrastructure-as-code tools (Terraform) to deploy services to Azure.

As you embark on this learning journey, this book will guide you through the process of deploying and developing generative artificial intelligence (Gen-AI) solutions using Azure OpenAI services on Microsoft Azure. Your active participation in this process is key to your success, and therefore, I packed this book with many hands-on labs to help you get through the learning process.

In this book, I will guide you on how to develop Gen-AI solutions using the Azure OpenAI platform, with a step-by-step approach to setting up the services from the ground up and deploying them to Microsoft Azure. Besides using the Azure SDK for .NET, we will also utilize the Postman API client to access Azure OpenAI services like Whisper (text to speech), DALL-E (image generation), and the latest GPT-4o model.

Before we get started with Azure OpenAI, let's focus on Azure SDK for .NET. SDK stands for software development kit, a collection of tools and libraries that help developers create applications for a specific platform or service (Azure).

© The Editor(s) (if applicable) and The Author(s),
under exclusive license to APress Media, LLC, part of Springer Nature 2024
S. Ifrah, *Getting Started with Azure OpenAI*, https://doi.org/10.1007/979-8-8688-0599-8_1

In most cases, an SDK contains an application programming interface (API) that defines how the developer can interact with a platform (Azure) using tools (.NET, C#, VC Code) that facilitate development and deployment.

In this book, we will use the term Azure SDKs to refer to the libraries that Microsoft provides for various Azure services, such as Azure Machine Learning, Azure Cognitive Services, Azure Bot Service, etc. The Azure SDKs are also available in different programming languages like Python, C#, Java, JavaScript, and more.

The Azure SDKs enable you to access the features and capabilities of Azure services from your code without having to deal with low-level details or complex protocols. With the Azure OpenAI SDK library, we can create, configure, train, deploy, and manage AI models on Azure and integrate them with other Azure services and applications.

In this chapter, I will focus on the theoretical part of Azure OpenAI and provide a lot of background that will help you understand the practical part of the book. In this chapter, you will understand the following concepts:

- Models

- Prompt engineering

- Service limits

- Capacity limits

- Cost of running an AI model

- Tokens

- Model servicing

About Azure and Azure OpenAI

Azure is Microsoft's cloud computing platform that offers a wide range of cloud services and solutions for developers and organizations of all sizes. Azure AI is a set of tools and services built into Azure that enable developers to build Gen-AI-based applications using the open source framework of OpenAI and deploy them in Azure.

OpenAI services deployed in Azure run on Azure's robust security and compliance infrastructure and enjoy the high availability and redundancy of Azure datacenter infrastructure that includes 60 regions and 160 datacenters worldwide.

OpenAI is a research and nonprofit organization that aims to create and promote friendly AI that can benefit humanity.

This book is designed to help you get started with Azure OpenAI and learn how to use its features and capabilities using the Azure SDK for .NET to create and deploy AI models for different scenarios.

In the book, we will use multiple programming tools like Azure CLI and Azure PowerShell to deploy the underlying infrastructure services Azure OpenAI uses.

By the end of this book, you will have a solid understanding of Azure OpenAI and the technical knowledge to set up the underlying Azure infrastructure needed for Azure OpenAI and Azure OpenAI services.

Azure AI vs. Azure OpenAI

Before we get started, we must first understand the big difference between the following two services:

- Azure AI

- Azure OpenAI

Azure AI Services

Azure AI Services, formally known as Cognitive Services, was first introduced in 2015 as a set of cloud-based services for developers and data scientists to build intelligent applications using Microsoft's artificial intelligence (AI) and machine learning (ML) capabilities.

Azure AI was launched in 2023 as a rebrand for the existing Cognitive Services suite, including the famous OpenAI.

OpenAI is a research organization founded in 2015 by a group of prominent entrepreneurs, investors, and scientists. The mission of OpenAI is to ensure that artificial intelligence (AI) can be developed in a safe and beneficial way for humanity without being constrained by profit motives or corporate agendas.

OpenAI's most notable projects and capabilities include

- ChatGPT – Large-scale language model (LLM) that generates text and engages in conversations

- DALL-E – LLM model that generates images from text descriptions

- Codex – LLM model that understands and generates code and what powers the GitHub Copilot service

- Whisper – LLM model for speech recognition that can transcribe and translate language to text

On top of the OpenAI Services, Azure AI Services also offers the following core AI Services:

- Azure AI Search – AI service that enables developers to add search capabilities to their applications

- Azure OpenAI – As discussed, a set of tools and services built into Azure that enable developers to use the open source framework OpenAI and deploy them in Azure.

- Bot Service – Enables developers to build, connect, test, and deploy intelligent bots

- Content Safety – AI service that helps detect and filter out potentially unsafe content

- Custom Vision – AI service that enables developers to build custom image classification models

- Document Vision – AI service that enables developers to extract information from documents

- Document Intelligence – AI service that enables developers to extract insights and information from documents

- Face – an AI service that enables developers to detect and analyze faces in images

- Language – an AI service that enables developers to process natural language text

- Speech – an AI service that enables developers to convert speech to text and vice versa

- Translator – an AI service that enables developers to translate text between languages

- Vision – an AI service that enables developers to analyze and understand images

We can use the Azure AI services using the following .NET packages available on NuGet.

In case you are new to .NET, Nuget is a package manager for .NET development, and it allows developers to install, update, and manage libraries and dependencies for their projects.

Packages are installed using the Dotnet CLI, PowerShell, VS Code, and package references. For example, we use the following command to install a NuGet package using the Dotnet CLI.

```
dotnet add package Azure.AI.OpenAI --version 1.0.0-beta.16
```

Nuget holds over 200,000 packages that can be accessed using Visual Studio, the dotnet CLI, or the Nuget website.

Table 1-1 shows the Azure AI packages.

Table 1-1. *Services*

Service Name	.NET Package Details
Azure AI Search	Azure.Search.Documents
Azure OpenAI	Azure.AI.OpenAI
Bot Service	Azure.ResourceManager.BotService
Content Safety	Azure.AI.ContentSafety
Custom Vision	Microsoft.Azure.CognitiveServices.Vision.CustomVision. Prediction Microsoft.Azure.CognitiveServices.Vision.CustomVision. Training
Document Vision	Azure.AI.Vision.Core
Document Intelligence	Azure.AI.DocumentIntelligence
Face	Microsoft.Azure.CognitiveServices.Vision.Face
Language	Azure.AI.TextAnalytics
Speech	Microsoft.CognitiveServices.Speech
Translator	Azure.AI.Translation.Document
Vision	Microsoft.Azure.CognitiveServices.Vision.ComputerVision

Azure OpenAI

Now that we know about the capabilities of Azure AI Services, it is time we understand the capabilities of Azure OpenAI. As explained in the previous section, Azure OpenAI is one of the AI services Azure AI offers.

The reason Azure OpenAI receives so much attention is that it offers OpenAI services under the Microsoft Azure umbrella and allows large organizations to take advantage of existing investments in Azure and develop OpenAI services without needing to make too many changes to their infrastructure or security and compliance policies.

Azure OpenAI offers Azure customers and .NET developers the option to use existing tools, libraries, and code to develop the most advanced AI capabilities developed by OpenAI.

The most common use case for Azure OpenAI is the Azure OpenAI On Your Data, where customers can use OpenAI capabilities on their data, which range from databases to documents and more.

Azure OpenAI also offers infrastructure capabilities like private networking, AI content filtering, and high availability of data centers.

Understanding Prompt Engineering and GPT Models

Prompt engineering is one of the most important concepts of working with OpenAI and other LLMs. Prompt engineering is writing effective inputs for language models like GPT-4 that can perform various natural language tasks.

An input prompt consists of a query that specifies the task and provides some context and a response, which is the model's output based on the query.

GPT-4 is a large-scale language model that uses deep neural networks to learn from a massive amount of data and generate natural language responses as output.

Large Language Models (LLMs)

LLMs are a category of models designed to understand and generate human language. They are characterized by their large number of parameters, which enable them to capture complex linguistic patterns and knowledge.

GPT Models

GPT models are a specific type of LLM developed by OpenAI. They are based on the Transformer architecture and are designed primarily for generative tasks, meaning they can generate coherent and contextually relevant text.

Key Differences Between LLMs and GPT

Specificity: All GPT models are LLMs, but not all LLMs are GPT models. GPT is a specific implementation within the broader category of LLMs.

Architecture: While GPT models use the Transformer architecture, other LLMs might use different variations or optimizations of the Transformer model.

Training Objectives: GPT models are generally trained with a focus on generative tasks, whereas other LLMs might be optimized for different objectives, such as bidirectional understanding in the case of BERT.

In short, while GPT models are a subset of LLMs known for their text generation capabilities, LLMs encompass a wider range of models designed for various NLP tasks.

Prompt Engineering Strategies

- Choose the right format and tone for the query and the response. The more specific the request, the output will be accurate.

- Provide enough context, be specific, and provide examples for the model to understand the task and the desired output.

- Experiment with different variations and combinations of queries and responses to find the right prompt.

- Always evaluate the model's outputs using external sources, metrics, fluency, diversity, and alignment with the task goals.

- Provide feedback regarding the outputs, and correct it to improve the model's learning and trustworthiness.

Prompt engineering is a must skill for working with GPT models and other LLMs because it helps produce the right results from an LLM.

Azure OpenAI Models

Azure OpenAI offers almost the same range of OpenAI models with the latest API version. It is also a good idea to consider each model's cost when working with models, as prices are not the same for all models.

Azure OpenAI offering includes access to the following models:

- GPT-4 and GPT-4 Turbo – The most powerful language models ever created, with billions of parameters and unprecedented speed and accuracy

- GPT-3.5 – A scaled-down version of GPT-4, still capable of generating high-quality natural language for a variety of domains and tasks

- Embeddings – A service that provides vector representations of words, sentences, and documents, enabling semantic similarity and clustering analysis

- DALL-E – A generative model that can create stunning images from natural language descriptions, such as "a cat wearing a bow tie" or "a snail made of harp"

- Whisper – A service that converts text to audio with a choice of voices, languages, and emotions

Using Azure OpenAI models works on the principle of using and accessing any REST API service and makes no difference if we are pointing to an OpenAI API endpoint or an Azure OpenAI API endpoint.

Azure OpenAI gives us access to the latest and newest OpenAI models like GPT-4, GPT-3.5 Turbo, and more. These models allow us to:

- Generate content

- Summarize text

- Use images with prompts

- Use semantic search

- Generate code and scripts

These services are available to us using the Azure OpenAI REST API endpoints or using the Azure SDKs. We can also use these services with Azure OpenAI Studio, which is a portal that allows us to use OpenAI services using a GUI interface. We will cover the OpenAI Studio later in the book.

Limits, Capacity, Context, and Tokens

One of the things we need to be aware of when working with LLMs is their limited capacity to process and generate text. Every LLM uses tokens to calculate words, subwords, or characters that can be combined to form words and sentences. That calculation is also used to calculate the cost of running an LLM.

When working with Azure OpenAI deployment, Azure allocates each subscription a service quota that provides a rate limit per model deployment in order to maintain service reliability.

A rate limit is calculated using the Tokens-Per-Minute (TPM) in multiples of 1000 the deployment consumes. For example, the GPT-4 model has a 40K TPM limit per deployment. On top of the Azure RPM limit, each model has a maximum request limit in tokens. Table 1-2 shows the list of GPT-4 models at the time of writing this book.

Table 1-2. *Max request limit*

Model ID	Max Request (Tokens)
gpt-4 (0314)	8,192 (8K)
gpt-4-32k (0314)	32,768 (32K)
gpt-4 (0613)	8,192 (8K)
gpt-4-32k (0613)	32,768 (32K)
gpt-4 (1106-Preview) GPT-4 Turbo Preview	Input: 128,000 (128K) Output: 4,096 (4K)
gpt-4 (0125-Preview)1GPT-4 Turbo Preview	Input: 128,000 (128K) Output: 4,096 (4K)
gpt-4 (vision-preview)2GPT-4 Turbo with Vision Preview	Input: 128,000 (128K) Output: 4,096 (4K)

Understanding Context and K

When working with models and as shown in Table 1-2, each model has a context limit defined by K. The K next to the number means "Killo" (thousand). When working with the gpt-4-32k model, the 32K means the model can use 32K tokens per context window (also known as session or conversation).

As explained earlier, a token in the context of GPT-4 represents a whole word or a subword. This means the model can generate a text with a maximum of 32K in a single conversation (also known as context window).

A context window refers to the maximum amount of text (in tokens) that the model can accept as input at one time. This also applies to the amount of output the model can return.

In practice, a 32K context window is a lot, giving the model a large amount of information for reference and output. It also allows us to input a very large amount of data to the model and produce an extensive amount of text.

The Benefits of Using a Large Context Window

When working with an 8K (default) and a 32K LLM model, we can easily understand the following main benefits of using a large (K) context window:

- Produce better results by inputting more information into the model and generating more information like results, etc.

- Broader reference – With a large context, the model can "remember" more information and retain more knowledge.

- Relevance – The more information the model has, the greater the relevance and accuracy of information it produces.

As AI continues to evolve and grow, the focus will be on the size of the context of new models in the upcoming years. More context means more capabilities and more processing power.

When working with models in the current environment, it is recommended to update the model you are working with to the latest model release. A new release means more tokens and up-to-date training data.

Training data (up to) in the context of LLM models refers to the dataset used to train the model. In the case of the gpt-4 (0314) model, the training data dataset is up to September 2021, which means the model doesn't know about events that took place after September 2021.

The latest GPT-4 model, gpt-4 (0125-preview), has a training data that goes up to December 2023. It also has a context window of 128K. This is a major improvement compared to the 0314 model and can make a huge difference to the results on an LLM application, not to mention the results the model can output.

Another point to consider is the retirement dates of the module; as of writing these lines, the 0314 model will be retired after July 5, 2024. For that reason, Azure introduced a feature that will automatically update models.

Cost of Azure OpenAI Models

As mentioned earlier, each model has a context limit and also a price, and choosing the right model is an important task. Just like selecting the size of an Azure Virtual Machine, we also need to take the same approach when working with OpenAI models.

Table 1-3 outlines the price of each OpenAI model Azure offers. Based on the needs of your application, you can select a model that gives your application the right context window and the right price.

The context window is the main factor affecting the price per 1K tokens. The larger the window, the higher the cost. If your application doesn't require a large context window, you might be better off selecting a cheaper model.

Table 1-3. *Model pricing*

Models	Context	Input (Per 1,000 Tokens)	Output (Per 1,000 Tokens)
GPT-3.5-Turbo-0125	16K	$0.0005	$0.0015
GPT-3.5-Turbo-Instruct	4K	$0.0015	$0.002
GPT-4-Turbo	128K	$0.01	$0.03
GPT-4-Turbo-Vision	128K	$0.01	$0.03
GPT-4	8K	$0.03	$0.06
GPT-4	32K	$0.06	$0.12

If you look at Table 1-3, you can see the price differences between each model. It is crucial you take into consideration the cost of the model when designing a Gen-I solution. Another factor that needs to be taken into consideration is the domain of the model; the GPT-3.5-Turbo-Instruct offers optimized instructions-based tasks, while the vision models can handle text and image capabilities.

If you are using an OpenAI model in a production environment, it is not recommended to use a preview model. In production workloads, always use nonpreview OpenAI models.

Count Tokens

Now that we understand the direct effect of the context window on the price we pay for using an OpenAI model, you probably want to have some control on the number of tokens you pass a model, not necessarily to monitor cost but more to prevent your application from hitting the model limit.

If you are using an 8K model and your application sends more than an 8K input prompt to the model, the result will be limited and maybe not complete.

To deal with both model tokens limit and Tokens-Per-Minute (TPM) imposed by Azure, we need to be aware of how many tokens we send to Azure OpenAI deployments.

Using the .NET `Microsoft.ML.Tokenizers` .NET library, we can count tokens before or after they are sent or received to an LLM model. In some cases, using a token counter is essential as we don't want to receive unaccepted results from the model because we sent an over-the-limit input.

Later in this book, we will show how to use the `Microsoft.ML.Tokenizers` .NET library to calculate tokens.

Versions and Updates

As Azure OpenAI and OpenAI introduce new capabilities and effectively, more LLM models are needed to keep their offerings up-to-date and make room for newer models. As a result, Azure retires and deprecates existing models.

Azure OpenAI terminology for the process of discontinued models is split into two:

- Retirement – This is the process of making a model unavailable.

- Depreciation – This is the process of making a model unavailable for new customers while maintaining it for existing customers.

When Azure OpenAI retires or makes a model deprecated, it will notify existing customers who use the model via email; however, make sure you check the Azure website for model servicing announcements.

Azure will notify customers 60 days before a model is retired and 30 days before depreciation.

Auto-update

If you select the current default version of a model, for example, GPT-4 version 0314, Azure will auto-update your deployment to the next default version of the GPT-4 model, which is 0613.

By using a current default version of a model, you are guaranteed to receive the latest capabilities Azure OpenAI offers for a model family.

Currently, Azure offers the following three update policies when choosing a model:

- Auto-update to default

- Upgrade when expired

- No auto-upgrade

By selecting one of the first two options, you are guaranteed a smooth update process without any downtime or outage for your application. I strongly recommend you avoid using the last option, which is essentially a manual update process.

Azure OpenAI Models Retirement Dates

Table 1-4 outlines the current models Azure OpenAI offers and the beginning of the retirement date (when a model stops working).

Some of these dates will not be relevant when this book is published; however, we can learn from the table how Azure OpenAI streamlines the retirement and provisioning of new and old OpenAI models.

Table 1-4. *Retirement dates*

Model	Version	Start Retirement Date
gpt-35-turbo	0301	June 13, 2024
gpt-35-turbogpt-35-turbo-16k	0613	July 13, 2024
gpt-35-turbo	1106	Nov 17, 2024
gpt-35-turbo	0125	Feb 22, 2025
gpt-4gpt-4-32k	0314	July 13, 2024
gpt-4gpt-4-32k	0613	Sep 30, 2024
gpt-4	1106-preview	Next default version
gpt-4	0125-preview	Next default version
gpt-4	Vision-preview	Next default version
gpt-3.5-turbo-instruct	0914	Sep 14, 2025
text-embedding-ada-002	2	April 3, 2025
text-embedding-ada-002	1	April 3, 2025
text-embedding-3-small		Feb 2, 2025
text-embedding-3-large		Feb 2, 2025

Azure OpenAI Models Deprecated Key Dates

Take a look at Table 1-5. It shows the deprecated history of Azure OpenAI models. A fascinating fact to notice is the gap between the deprecation date and the retirement date, which is 12 months. This is a long period that gives Azure customers more than enough time to prepare to update their deployment.

It also shows the commitment Microsoft has to customers and how it works well for large enterprises that run critical applications in Azure and need a long prep time to update.

Table 1-5. *Deprecated models*

Model	Deprecation Date	Retirement Date	Suggested Replacement
Ada	July 6, 2023	July 5, 2024	babbage-002
babbage	July 6, 2023	July 5, 2024	babbage-002
Curie	July 6, 2023	July 5, 2024	davinci-002
davinci	July 6, 2023	July 5, 2024	davinci-002
text-ada-001	July 6, 2023	July 5, 2024	gpt-35-turbo-instruct
text-babbage-001	July 6, 2023	July 5, 2024	gpt-35-turbo-instruct
text-curie-001	July 6, 2023	July 5, 2024	gpt-35-turbo-instruct
text-davinci-002	July 6, 2023	July 5, 2024	gpt-35-turbo-instruct
text-davinci-003	July 6, 2023	July 5, 2024	gpt-35-turbo-instruct
code-cushman-001	July 6, 2023	July 5, 2024	gpt-35-turbo-instruct
code-davinci-002	July 6, 2023	July 5, 2024	gpt-35-turbo-instruct

(continued)

Table 1-5. (*continued*)

Model	Deprecation Date	Retirement Date	Suggested Replacement
text-similarity-ada-001	July 6, 2023	July 5, 2024	text-embedding-3-small
text-similarity-babbage-001	July 6, 2023	July 5, 2024	text-embedding-3-small
text-similarity-curie-001	July 6, 2023	July 5, 2024	text-embedding-3-small
text-similarity-davinci-001	July 6, 2023	July 5, 2024	text-embedding-3-small
text-search-ada-doc-001	July 6, 2023	July 5, 2024	text-embedding-3-small
text-search-ada-query-001	July 6, 2023	July 5, 2024	text-embedding-3-small
text-search-babbage-doc-001	July 6, 2023	July 5, 2024	text-embedding-3-small
text-search-babbage-query-001	July 6, 2023	July 5, 2024	text-embedding-3-small
text-search-curie-doc-001	July 6, 2023	July 5, 2024	text-embedding-3-small
text-search-curie-query-001	July 6, 2023	July 5, 2024	text-embedding-3-small
text-search-davinci-doc-001	July 6, 2023	July 5, 2024	text-embedding-3-small

(*continued*)

Table 1-5. (*continued*)

Model	Deprecation Date	Retirement Date	Suggested Replacement
text-search-davinci-query-001	July 6, 2023	July 5, 2024	text-embedding-3-small
code-search-ada-code-001	July 6, 2023	July 5, 2024	text-embedding-3-small
code-search-ada-text-001	July 6, 2023	July 5, 2024	text-embedding-3-small
code-search-babbage-code-001	July 6, 2023	July 5, 2024	text-embedding-3-small
code-search-babbage-text-001	July 6, 2023	July 5, 2024	text-embedding-3-small

Azure OpenAI Subscription Limits

As discussed earlier in brief, besides each model token's limit, Azure also has a rate limit/quota that applies on a subscription level and limits the number of Tokens-Per-Minute (TPM) a deployment can process.

While each deployment has a TPM limit, each subscription has a global quota that all the deployments are limited to. When the number of deployments reaches the global quota, no more deployments can be created until you reduce the RPM per deployment or delete deployments.

On a deployment level, we have the option to set a limit below the allowable limit, as shown in Figure 1-1.

In Figure 1-1, I have set the TPM to 10K, while the region limit for GPT-4 deployments is up to 40K. It is also a good idea to set a lower limit for nonproduction deployments and prevent development deployments effecting the global quote of the subscription.

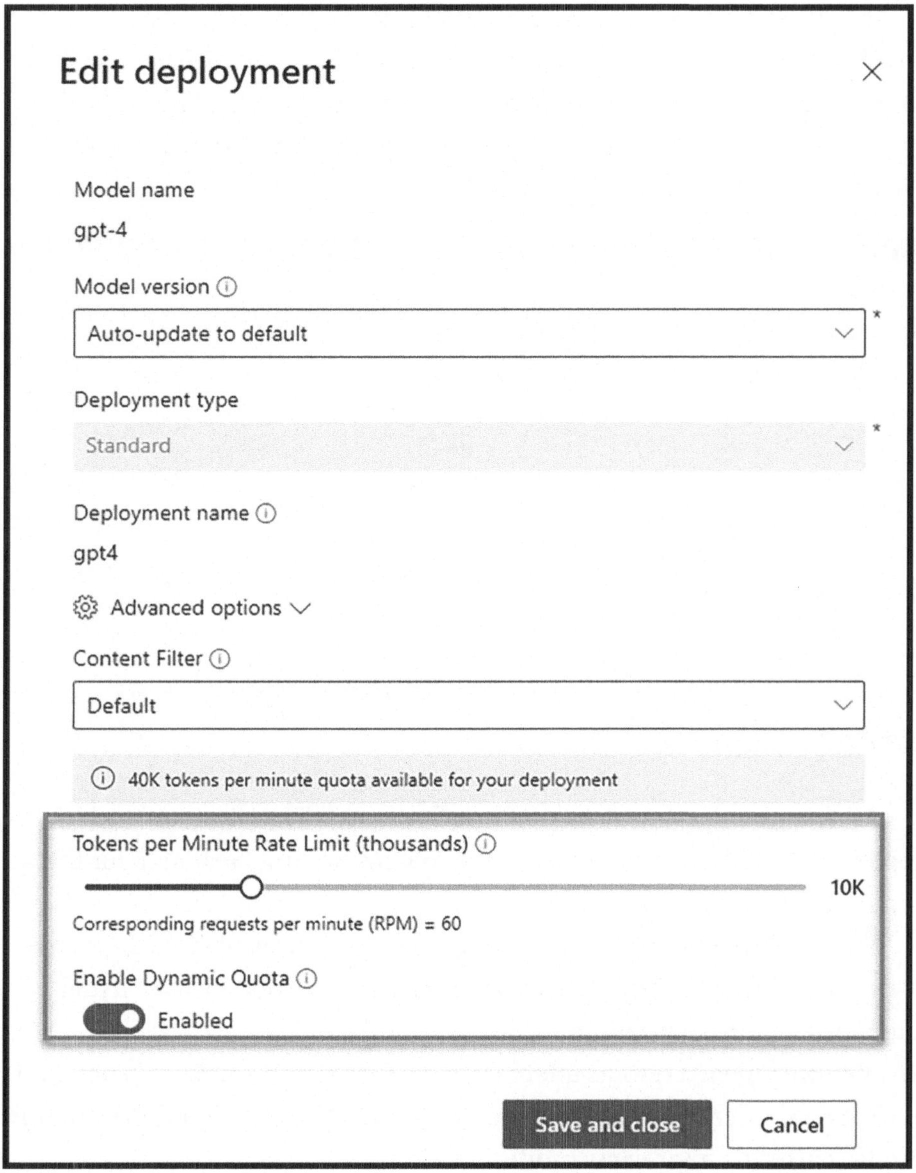

Figure 1-1. *TPM limit*

It is important to note that the TPM limit can be set pre- and postdeployment using the Azure OpenAI Studio portal, which we will cover later in this book. At any given time, we can view and monitor the overall quota of our tenant and view how many TPM each deployment uses. Figure 1-2 shows the Quotas screen.

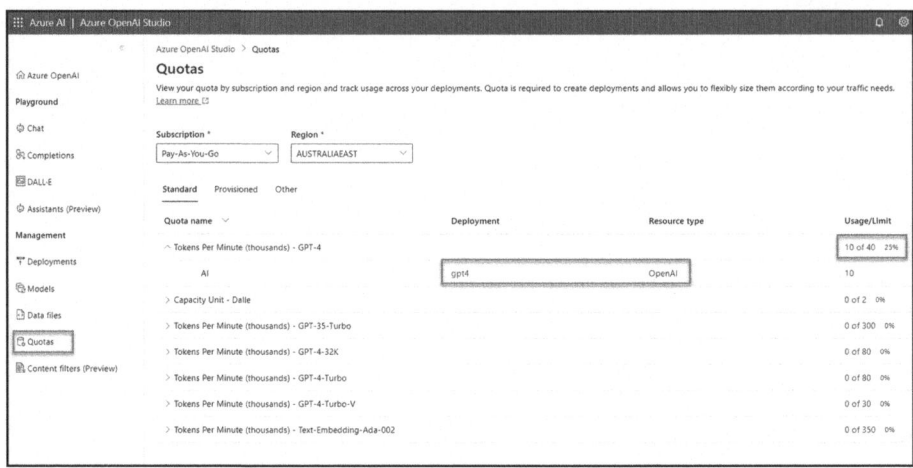

Figure 1-2. *Quotas*

As best practice, it is recommended you set a TPM limit on each deployment that is not necessarily the maximum limit available for the deployment.

Setting TPM limit and managing deployment capacity for AI models is the same as managing capacity of other Azure resources like virtual machines, storage, and more.

If Azure OpenAI quotas affect your resources and you have a need for more Azure, offer organizations the option to use Azure OpenAI Dynamic Quota (currently in preview mode).

Dynamic Quota

Azure OpenAI Dynamic Quota allows organizations to take advantage of unused capacity in Azure OpenAI and extend the overall quota set on your subscription. To use Dynamic Quota in our deployments, we need to enable it on each deployment, as shown in Figure 1-3.

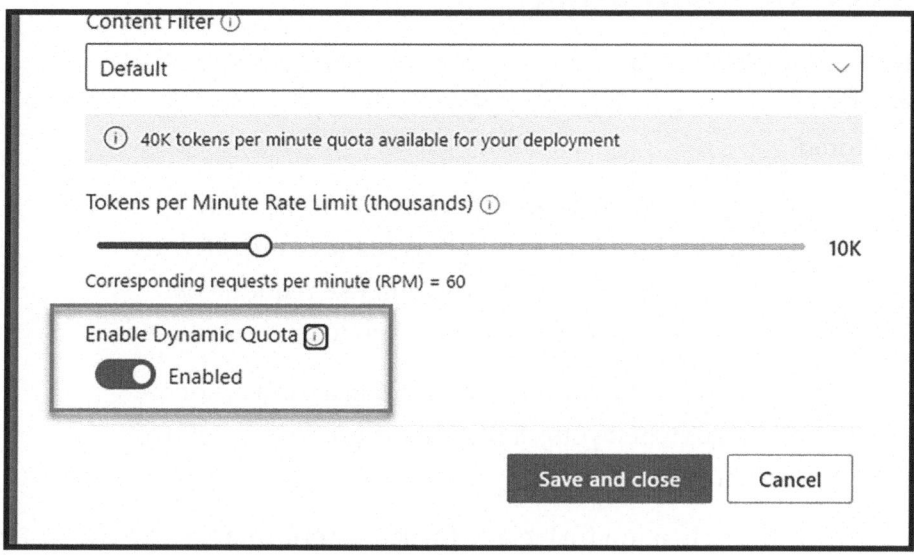

Figure 1-3. *Enable Dynamic Quota*

Monitoring Capacity

As you deploy more and more OpenAI models, you should monitor the usage and capacity of each deployment.

Monitoring OpenAI resources has two main benefits. First, it helps us understand and ensure that deployments have enough capacity at a subscription level and also at a deployment level.

It helps us detect unauthorized usage of API key or if the application is configured in a way that it consumes too many tokens, effectively increasing the overall cost of Azure.

Best Practices for Azure OpenAI Resource Monitoring

The following list of items outlines a few best practices you should follow when working with Azure OpenAI and ensure resources are being monitored:

- Use the Azure portal or the Azure CLI to view the metrics and logs of your deployments. Azure offers a large set of metrics to choose from like requests per second, average latency, errors, and tokens consumed.

- Set up alerts and notifications to receive emails or SMS messages when your deployments exceed predefined thresholds.

- Use Application Insights to track the performance and availability of your applications that use Azure OpenAI. If the application fails, it might be related to the Azure OpenAI service.

- Use Azure Monitor to create dashboards and reports that show the health and status of your Azure OpenAI resources and subscriptions.

The following screenshot, shown in Figure 1-4, shows the monitoring panel of an Azure OpenAI resource.

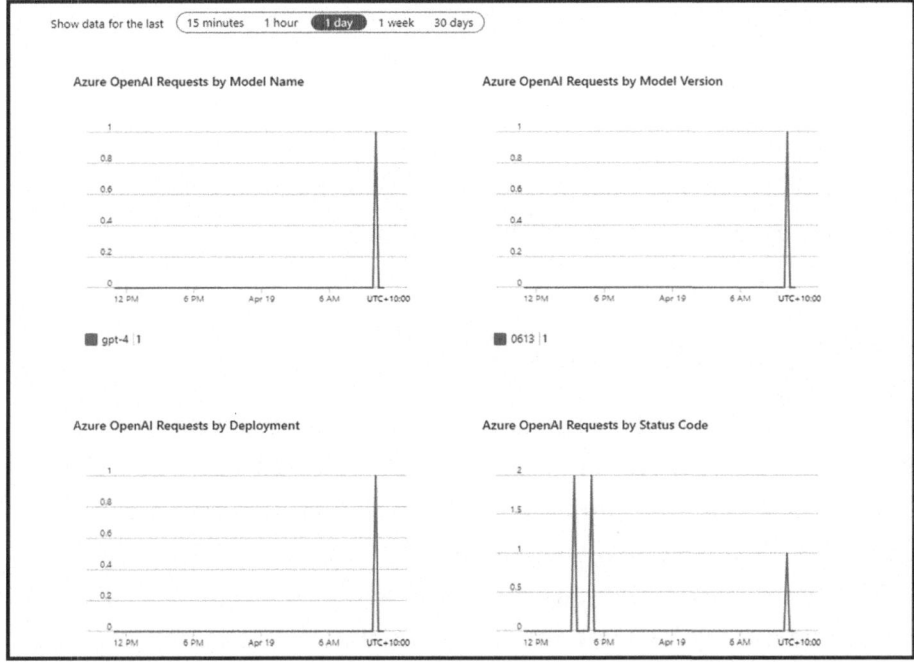

Figure 1-4. *Azure Monitor for an Azure OpenAI resource*

Each Azure OpenAI resource has a dedicated Microsoft Azure Monitor section with metrics that measure the health of an Azure OpenAI deployment.

```
https://learn.microsoft.com/en-us/azure/ai-services/openai/
how-to/quota?tabs=rest
```

Programming Languages

As mentioned earlier, this book will focus on using Azure OpenAI with Microsoft.NET; however, it's important to note that the Azure OpenAI SDK is available in the following programming languages:

- C#

- Go

- Java

- JavaScript

- Python

Since this book is for .NET, we will use C# as the underlying programming language with .NET 7 and above.

Azure OpenAI REST API

The Azure SDK for .NET and all other SDKs use the Azure REST API service. The Azure Representational State Transfer (REST) API service acts as an endpoint that allows us to run operations that create, retrieve, update, and delete Azure resources and services.

The Azure OpenAI, like all other Azure Services, has a REST API Service that the .NET SDK communicates with. The link below outlines the API and all the operations that we can use against an Azure OpenAI endpoint.

`https://learn.microsoft.com/en-us/rest/api/azureopenai/operation-groups?view=rest-azureopenai-2024-03-01-preview`

The latest generally available version of the Azure OpenAPI is 2024-02-01. The preview version is 2024-03-01-preview.

If you decide to use the REST API directly in a production environment, it is recommended you use the GA version.

The REST API service version drop-down menu lists all the preview and GA versions. The versions that do not contain the -preview text are GA versions. Like with models, Azure also retires API versions. Figure 1-5 shows the REST API service page for the Azure OpenAI service.

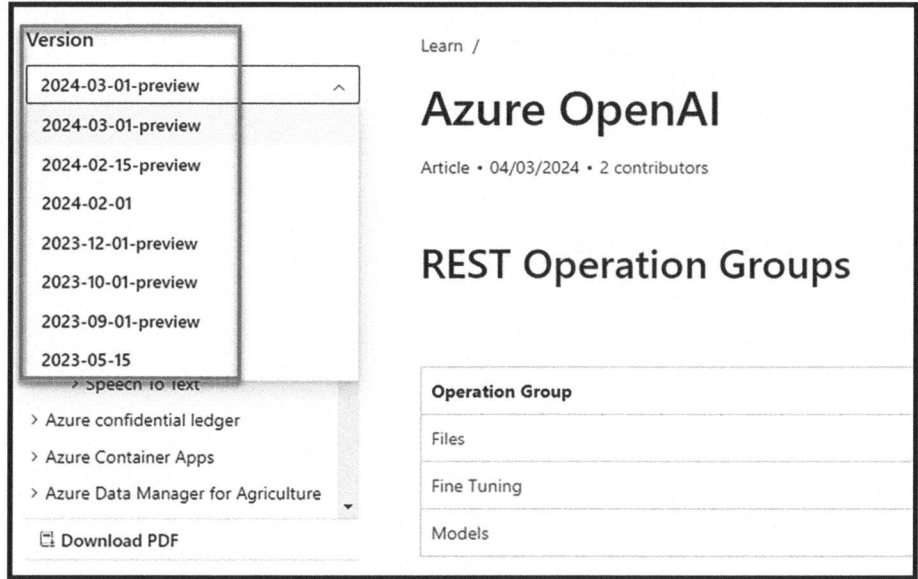

Figure 1-5. *Azure OpenAI REST service page*

On a side note, I would like to mention that you can also use the Azure OpenAI service with REST API tools like Postman to connect to an Azure OpenAI endpoint and consume the service.

Getting a Base Model Using REST API

The following REST API call (GET) to the Azure OpenAI service will list all the AI models an account owns.

GET `https://aoairesource.openai.azure.com/openai/models?api-version=2024-03-01-preview`

If you look at the API call, you will see that at the end of the URL, we reference the API version, which is `api-version=2024-03-01-preview.`

The REST API response is returned using a JSON format, and it is listed as follows (I shortened it to just a few models).

```json
{
  "data": [
    {
      "status": "succeeded",
      "capabilities": {
        "fine_tune": false,
        "inference": true,
        "completion": false,
        "chat_completion": false,
        "embeddings": false
      },
      "lifecycle_status": "preview",
      "deprecation": {
        "inference": 1721001600
      },
      "id": "dall-e-3-3.0",
      "created_at": 1691712000,
      "object": "model"
    },
    {
      "status": "succeeded",
      "capabilities": {
        "fine_tune": false,
        "inference": true,
        "completion": true,
        "chat_completion": true,
        "embeddings": false
```

The point that I'm trying to make here is that the Azure REST API is what drives all programming tools we use to deploy and manage Azure services, and behind the scenes, all tools are using the Azure REST API service.

For more information about the Azure REST API service, visit `https://learn.microsoft.com/en-us/rest/api/azure/`.

Azure OpenAI Assistants vs. Chat Completions

OpenAI Chat Completions LLM models were designed to accept input in the form of text (also known as prompts) and provide output in the form of natural language, images, and code.

These models allow building applications, services, and solutions that are based on text generation and are capable of

- Writing code and scripts

- Generating content and documents

- Analyzing text

- Detecting languages

- Detecting mode and sentiments

- Answering general questions

The core function of the chat completion models is to take a list of messages and provide an output.

The downfall of the Chat Completions models is that they are stateless, which means that they do not save or remember the state information of the chat. To overcome that limitation, developers had to write complex code that managed the chat and conversation history which increased the development effort of LLM applications.

Assistants API

The latest OpenAI LLM model, Assistants API, offers a stateful solution for LLM applications and resolves all the challenges developers face when working with Chat Completions models. The new API which is still in preview mode offers advanced capabilities and less development effort because by default without any extra codding the model supports the following:

- Persistent chat history (out-of-the-box)

- Auto management of max tokens context window

- Access to Code Interpreter tools

- Access to File Search

- Access to Function Calling

Components of the Assistants API

The following list outlines all the components that make the Assistants API and help us create an LLM solution:

- Assistant – A personalized AI that combines Azure OpenAI models with tools.

- Thread – A chat session between an Assistant and a user. Threads keep Messages and automatically manage shortening to fit content into a model's context.

- Message – A piece of communication that an Assistant or a user makes. Messages can have text, images, and other files. Messages are kept as a list on the Thread.

- Run – When an Assistant is activated to start running according to the Thread's content, it is called a Run. The Assistant uses its settings and the Messages in the Thread to do tasks by using models and tools.

- Run Step – A list of actions the Assistant performed as part of a Run.

In addition to the above components, the API can access a Code Interpreter. The Code Interpreter tool is made of a Python sandbox environment that allows the API to write and run Python code in the forms of functions, calculations, and more. The API is also smart enough to rerun the code until it works and detect when the code fails.

Another tool that is also available with the Assistants API is Function Calling; with Function Calling, we can describe a needed function to the Assistants API, and it will return a function with the argument the function will take.

The Assistances API version is available with the following Azure REST API version: `version=2024-02-15-preview`.

Handy Resources

Before we wrap up this chapter, I would like to add a few references (Table 1-6) to the resources I mentioned in this chapter. The following references are the official documentation from Azure and OpenAI.

Table 1-6. *Handy resources*

Resource Name	URL
Azure OpenAI Documentation	`https://learn.microsoft.com/en-us/azure/ai-services/openai/`
Azure OpenAI REST API	`https://learn.microsoft.com/en-us/rest/api/azureopenai/operation-groups?view=rest-azureopenai-2024-03-01-preview`
OpenAI Documentation	`https://platform.openai.com/docs/introduction`
Azure OpenAI .NET SDK	`https://learn.microsoft.com/en-us/dotnet/api/azure.ai.openai?view=azure-dotnet-preview`

Chapter Summary

In this chapter, we covered the theoretical part of Azure OpenAI without getting into the how-to and the technical details required to get started. The goal of this chapter is to give you enough information about Azure OpenAI so that when we get to the hands-on chapters of this book, you will understand what you're doing.

CHAPTER 2

Install Tools (Azure CLI, Azure PowerShell, VS Code, Copilot)

In Chapter 1, we covered the theoretical part of Azure OpenAI and OpenAI. The focus was to understand the service offering, and the services are different from one another.

This chapter will highlight the crucial role of the tools and services we need to connect, create, and develop AI services hosted in Azure OpenAI.

In this chapter, we will do the following:

- Create an Azure Account and subscription.

- Request access to Azure OpenAI Service.

- Install .NET.

- Install Visual Studio Code.

- Install Visual Studio Code extensions needed.

- Install Visual Studio.

- Install Azure PowerShell.

© The Editor(s) (if applicable) and The Author(s),
under exclusive license to APress Media, LLC, part of Springer Nature 2024
S. Ifrah, *Getting Started with Azure OpenAI*, https://doi.org/10.1007/979-8-8688-0599-8_2

- Install Azure CLI.

- Install Terraform.

- Install Postman.

- Install Git.

All the labs in this book will work on Windows, macOS, and Linux, so you can use any operating system you feel comfortable working with. Please note that Visual Studio is more of a Windows application, and the macOS version is scheduled for retirement after August 31, 2024.

If you are on MacOS or Linux, please use VS Code. I will use VS Code on both macOS and Windows throughout this book.

If you are on a Windows machine, you can also use the Windows Subsystem for Linux (WSL) with VS Code and install the Linux version of the tools inside WSL.

Create a Microsoft Azure Account

To use Azure, we must have a valid (not trial) account and subscription with administrative rights or, at minimum, contributor rights to the subscription.

If you do not have an account, head to Azure.com and create a valid subscription. You must not use a trial account with free credits because a trial account has many limitations that will prevent you from completing the labs shown in this book.

If you are new to Azure, you can sign up for a free account and receive a $200 credit for 30 days. I don't recommend using the free account to complete the labs in this book, but it is possible to use other services under the free offer.

All labs in this book are suitable for Azure subscriptions with pay-as-you-go corporate subscriptions free from limitations.

Figure 2-1 shows the Azure.com home page.

Click the Get Started link to start registering a new subscription.

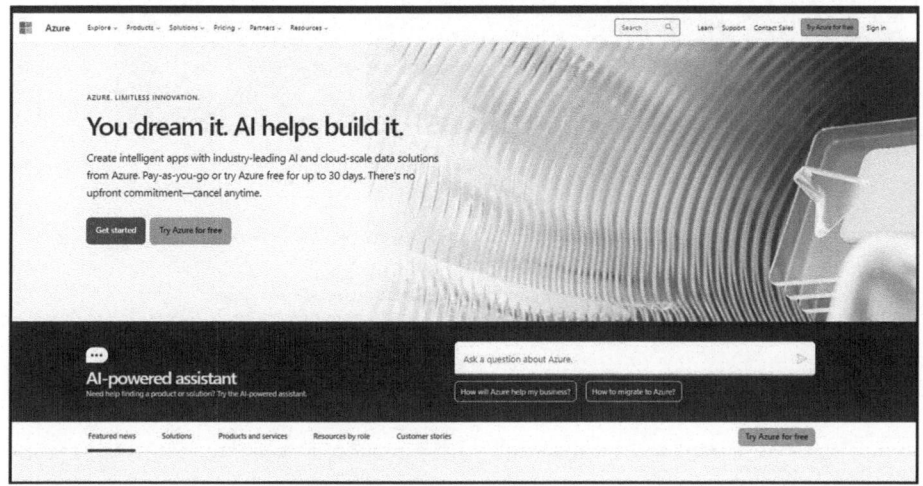

Figure 2-1. *Azure.com home page*

Once you create a new subscription and have an account, you can log in to Azure using the following URL, `https://portal.azure.com/`, where all the Azure services are located.

If you are new to the platform, I recommend you log in to the Azure portal and explore Azure's services.

In case you need to get more familiar with Microsoft Azure, please review the latest Apress books on the topic and my *Getting Started with Containers in Azure* book.

Request Access to Azure OpenAI Service

Due to the popularity of Azure OpenAI, access to the service is limited and requires approval from Microsoft before access is granted. To get access to Azure OpenAI, fill the application form in the following URL `https://aka.ms/oai/access` and as shown in Figure 2-2.

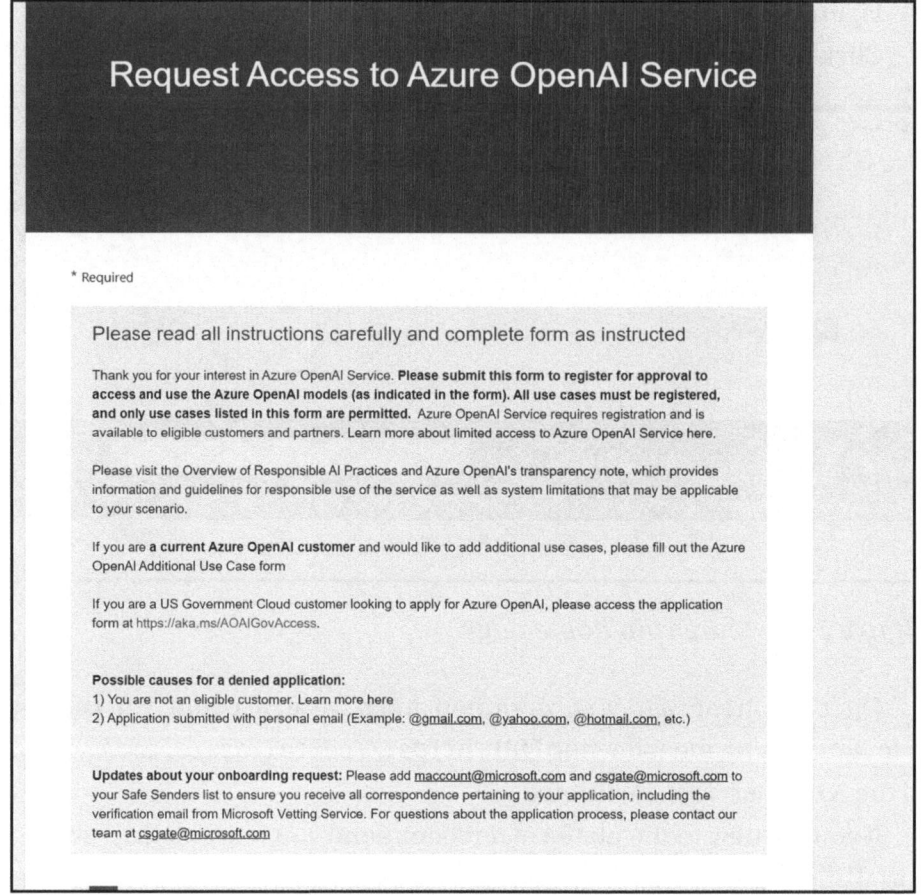

Figure 2-2. *Request access to Azure OpenAI*

Before applying, apply for it with a company email address, not a personal one like outlook.com.

You will also need to provide the subscription ID of your Azure subscription, which you will find in the Azure portal under Subscriptions. If you have multiple subscriptions, ensure you provide the correct ID.

You can add up to three subscriptions in a single application. After submitting the application, wait for approval, which can take anywhere between days to weeks.

Azure SDK for .NET

As discussed in Chapter 1, The Azure SDKs are available in several languages, and in this book, we will focus on the .NET SDK. This book assumes that you're already familiar with .NET and C#. However, if you don't, I recommend you review the *Pro C# 10 with .NET 6* book to get familiar with the language and framework.

The Azure SDK for .NET allows us to create, use, and access Azure services from almost any .NET application. We use NuGet packages for specific Azure services, as discussed in Chapter 1. Below are a few use cases in which we can use the Azure SDK for . NET:

- Create an LLM application to perform natural language processing, computer vision, or speech recognition on user inputs or uploaded files.

- Use Azure AI services to extract information from web pages or text.

- Download files.

- Manage Azure resources.

The above are just a few simple examples, but we can also use Azure to host our applications or integrate Azure AI search inside an existing application.

The advantage of using the .NET SDK is that it allows us to access Azure services using existing tools we are already using and familiar with without investing time in learning new languages.

Package List

As mentioned before, the Azure SDK for .NET is made of service-specific NuGet packages and a Core package called Azure.Core that acts as a dependency. You can view the package list in the following URL for reference, as shown in Figure 2-3.

https://learn.microsoft.com/en-us/dotnet/azure/sdk/packages

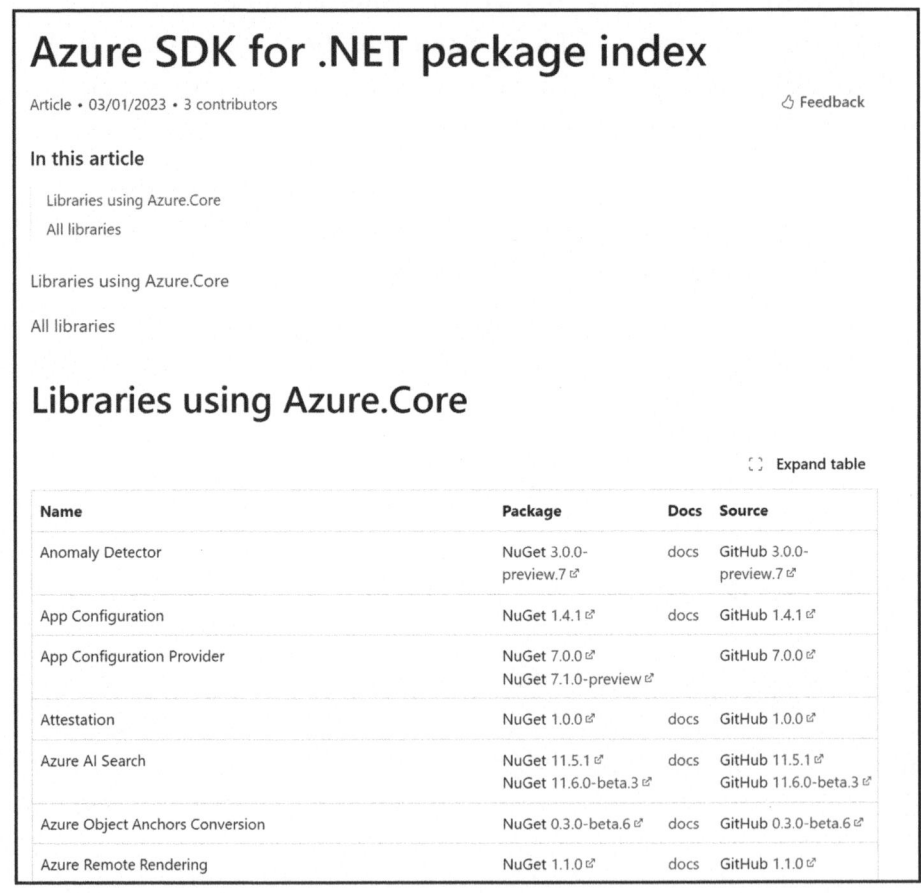

Figure 2-3. *Azure SDK for .NET packages*

As of writing this book, the SDK has 667 packages available.

If you wonder why there are so many packages available and why Microsoft didn't package the SDK into a small number of packages, the answer is that more packages mean a lighter footprint and more security, and it allows Microsoft to deliver updates quickly.

Let's continue with setting up our working environment and tools.

Install .NET

In this section, we will go over the installation process of .NET. In a nutshell, .NET is a free, open source, cross-platform development platform for the development of almost any application. With .NET, we can develop the following applications:

- Console applications

- Web application

- Mobile application

- Desktop application

- Games

- Function application

In this book, we will install the latest .NET version, which is .NET 8.0, with an end support date of November 10, 2026. The installation process is very simple. You can download .NET by visiting to the following URL `https://dotnet.microsoft.com/` and follow the instructions to download .NET, as shown in Figure 2-4.

Figure 2-4. *.NET home page*

Once you download .NET 8, head to the following URL `https://dotnet.microsoft.com/en-us/download/dotnet/8.0` and download the ASP.NET Core Runtime, as shown in Figure 2-5.

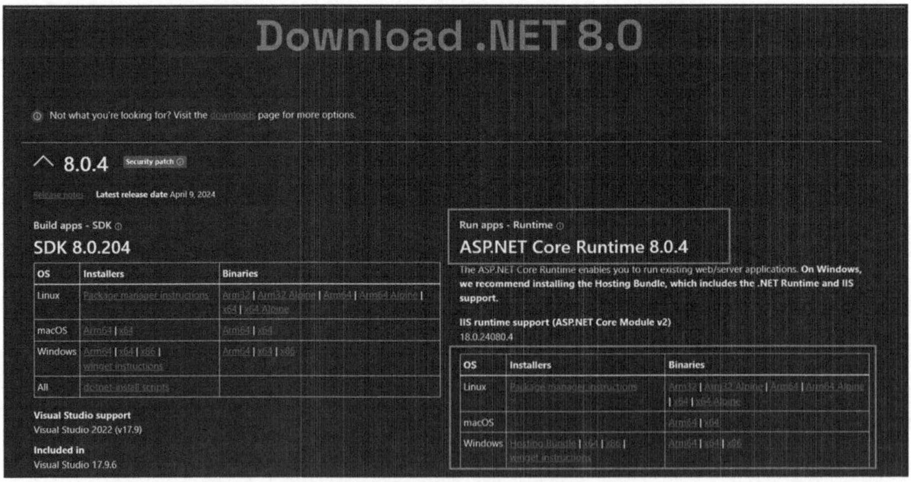

Figure 2-5. *Download ASP.NET Core Runtime*

Windows WinGet

In case you prefer to download .NET, on a Windows machine programmatically, you can download .NET using the following WinGet command.

```
Winget install Microsoft.DotNet.SDK.8
Winget install Microsoft.DotNet.AspNetCore.8
```

In case you are unfamiliar with WinGet, Windows Package Manager (WinGet) is a built-in Windows operating system (10 and above) package manager that allows us to use the command-line interface to download software packages.

Visual Studio Code

To complete the deployments and examples shown in this book, we will use Visual Studio Code (VS Code). VS Code is a lightweight source code editor that runs on all major operating systems and comes with built-in support for many programming languages.

The power of VS Code comes from its massive ecosystem of extensions that allow us to extend the editor's capabilities beyond just a source code editor. With VS Code extensions, we can

- Connect to remote hosts using Remote SSH

- Use Jupyter notebooks to run code

- Use Docker to deploy and manage containers

- Use GitHub Copilot

- Provide full PowerShell language support

- Deploy resources directly to Azure using the Azure extension

41

Install VS Code

To get started with VS Code and VS Code extensions, open the following URL https://code.visualstudio.com and download the latest stable release for your operating system as shown in Figure 2-6.

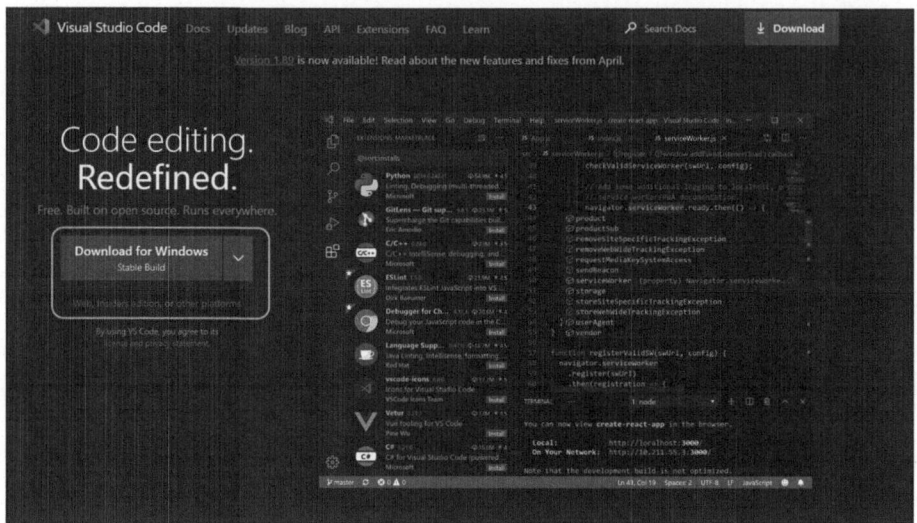

Figure 2-6. *Download VS Code*

Once you download VS Code, go through the installation process.

Install Extensions

After installing VS Code, let's install a few extensions that will make our life easier. To install extensions

Open VS Code Console

Click the Extension icon as shown in Figure 2-7

Figure 2-7. *VS Code extensions*

We use the search box in the main extension side menu to search for an extension.

Let's go ahead and go over the steps that are required to install an extension.

From the extensions search box, type the name of the extension you are looking for. In Figure 2-8, I'm looking for all the Azure extensions.

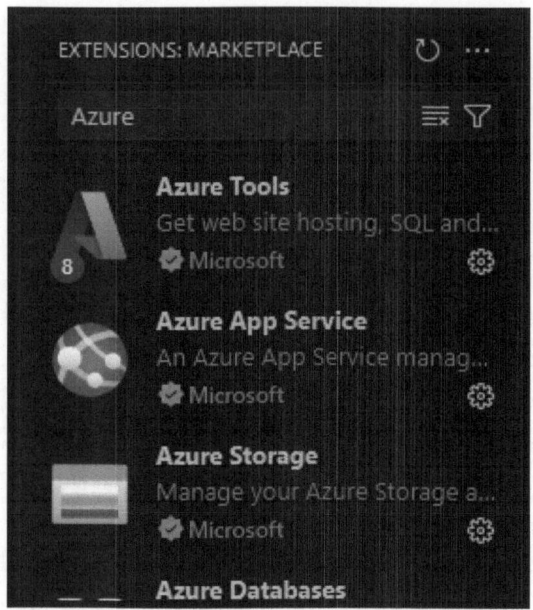

Figure 2-8. Search for an extension

Click the extension name.

Click install as shown in Figure 2-9.

Figure 2-9. Install and extension

Extensions List

Now that you know how to install extensions, go ahead and install the following extensions. Some of them are optional, but I do recommend you install them.

Extension Name	Details
Azure Account	A shared VS Code extension for logging in and managing subscriptions
Git Copilot	Your AI coding assistant
Git Copilot Chat	Copilot-based AI features for chatting
Jupyter	Jupyter notebook support, Intellisense, debugging, and more for interactive programming and computing
WSL	Use Visual Studio Code's features with any folder in the WSL
Azure CLI Tools	Resources for creating and executing Azure CLI commands
Azure Tools	This extension from Microsoft lets you access website hosting, SQL and MongoDB data, Docker Containers, Serverless Functions, and more on Azure, all within VS Code
Bicep	Bicep language support for Visual Studio Code
C#	Basic language features for C#
C# Dev Kit	Microsoft's official extension for C#
HashiCorp Terraform	Color-coded and suggested syntax for Terraform
PowerShell	Use Visual Studio Code to create PowerShell scripts, commands, and modules
Remote SSH	Use SSH to access any folder on a different machine and enjoy all the features of VS Code
Remote – SSH: Editing Configuration Files	Modify SSH settings files

Visual Studio 2022

Another great editor I would like to recommend you use if you're on a Windows machine is Visual Studio. Visual Studio is the world's number one integrated development environment (IDE) tool that offers end-to-end software development cycles in one place.

Visual Studio comes in the following editions.

Edition Name	Offer
Community	Free
Professional	Not free
Enterprise	Not free

The Community edition is freely used by the following:

- Individual developers

- Classroom learning

- Academic research

- Open source projects

All other use cases will require a paid edition.

To install Visual Studio, go to `https://visualstudio.microsoft.com/` and scroll down to the download section as shown in Figure 2-10.

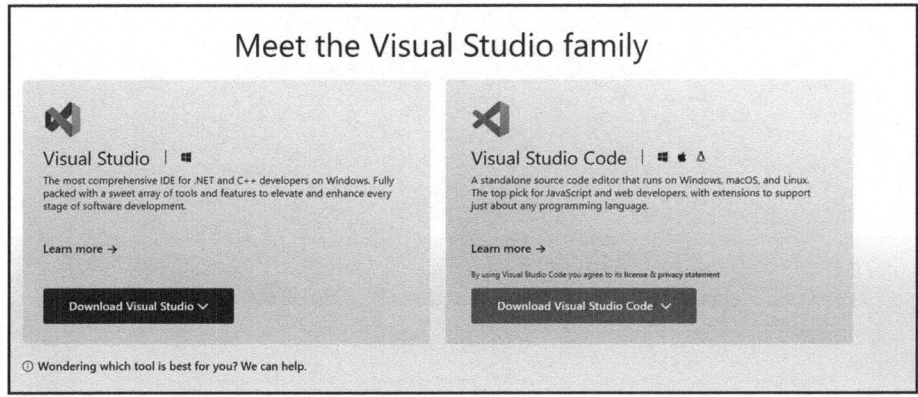

Figure 2-10. *Download Visual Studio*

If you are not sure which version to download, click the **Wondering which tool is best for you?** link as shown in Figure 2-11. If you select your OS machine type and programming language and use case, you will see which version is recommended for you to install.

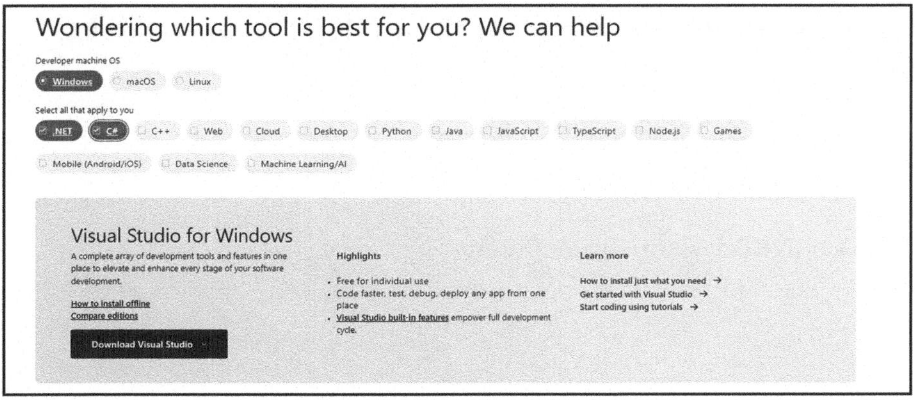

Figure 2-11. *Visual Studio version*

To install Visual Studio, click the download button shown in Figure 2-11 or use the following download URL `https://visualstudio.microsoft.com/downloads/#picker` as shown in Figure 2-12.

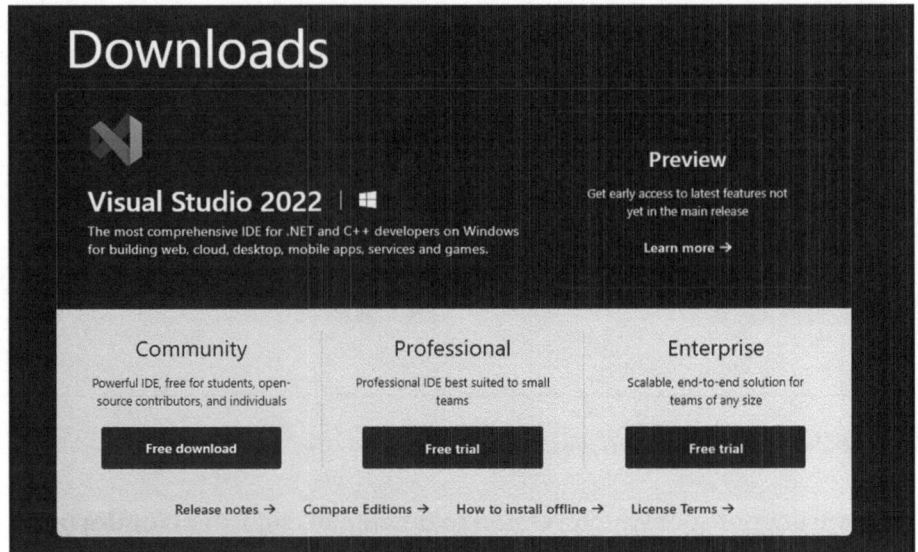

Figure 2-12. *Download Visual Studio 2022*

To install Visual Studio, start the installation process, and in the Workloads section screen (shown in Figure 2-13), select the following workloads:

- ASP.NET and web development

- Azure development

- .NET desktop development

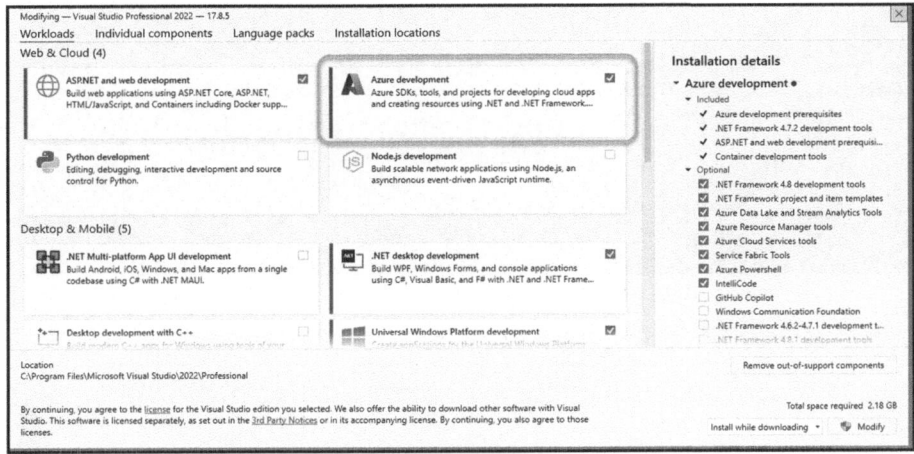

Figure 2-13. *Visual Studio Workloads*

Wait for the installation to finish.

Visual Studio 2022 Preview

If you like Visual Studio and would like to try and use the latest features before their official release, you can install and try the Preview edition of Visual Studio.

The Preview edition is installed side-by-side with previous releases that are installed on the machine. The only requirement is that you have enough disk space on your machine to accommodate all the editions.

To install Visual Studio Preview, go to the following URL and download the installation file. Figure 2-13a shows the main page.

```
https://visualstudio.microsoft.com/vs/preview/
```

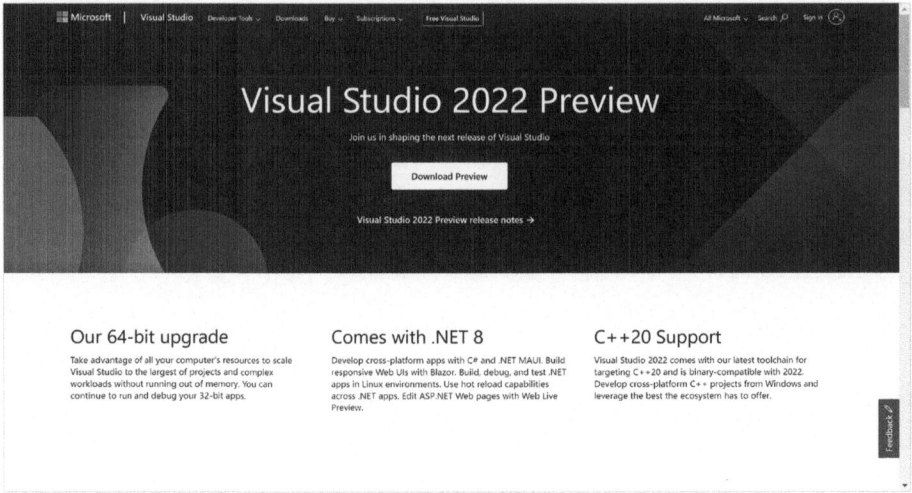

Figure 2-13a. *Visual Studio 2022 Preview*

Install Azure PowerShell

Azure PowerShell allows us to manage, administer, and deploy Azure resources using the PowerShell command line. Azure PowerShell, also known as Az PowerShell, is capable of managing almost any Azure service.

Since PowerShell is an open platform tool, we can use Az PowerShell on all major operating systems and from Azure Cloud Shell.

To install the latest version of Azure PowerShell, open the following URL: `https://github.com/Azure/azure-powershell/releases`.

The URL belongs to the Azure PowerShell open source project on GitHub and offers details about each version, including preview releases.

From the releases page, scroll down to the Assets section as shown in Figure 2-14.

Select and download the installer for your operating system.

▼ Assets 7		
🗍Az-Cmdlets-11.6.0.38526-x64.msi	92.3 MB	last week
🗍Az-Cmdlets-11.6.0.38526-x86.msi	89 MB	last week
🗍Az-Cmdlets-latest.tar.gz	92.8 MB	last week
🗍az-ps-latest.csv	24.4 KB	last week
🗍index.json	2.72 MB	last week
🗍Source code (zip)		2 weeks ago
🗍Source code (tar.gz)		2 weeks ago

Figure 2-14. *Az PowerShell assets*

Using the following commands on a Windows machine, you can also download Azure PowerShell directly from the PowerShell command line.

```
Get-ExecutionPolicy -List
Set-ExecutionPolicy -ExecutionPolicy RemoteSigned -Scope
CurrentUser
Install-Module -Name Az -Repository PSGallery -Force
```

Note   You would run the following command on a Linux or macOS operating system with PowerShell installed.

```
pwsh
Install-Module -Name Az -Repository PSGallery -Force
```

Sign In to Azure Using Azure PowerShell

To log in to Azure from the Azure PowerShell module, follow the following steps:

Open PowerShell (pwsh on Linux or macOS).

Issue to following command to connect and login to Azure.

```
Connect-AzAccount
```

Running the above command will open a web browser asking you to authenticate to Azure. If you prefer to open the browser or if you are on WSL, use the following command, which will provide you with a link and a code to enter after you authenticate to Azure.

```
Connect-AzAccount -UseDeviceAuthentication
```

I personally prefer to use the second option; however, this is up to you.

If you have more than one Azure subscription, you can set the subscription you would like to work with using the following cmdlet.

```
Set-AzContext -Subscription "pay-as-you-go"
```

To see which subscription Azure PowerShell is using, run the following cmdlet:

```
Get-AzContext | fl
```

The output will provide the following information about the subscription:

- Name
- Account
- Environment
- Subscription
- Tenant
- TokenCache
- VersionProfile
- ExtendedProperties : {}

To view all available resources deployed on your subscription, run the following command:

```
Get-AzResource
```

The output will show each resource and provide information about the following properties:

- Name

- ResourceGroupName

- ResourceType

- Location

- ResourceId

- Tags

Install Azure CLI

Another command-line tool that allows us to manage Microsoft Azure programmatically is the Azure Command-Line Interface (CLI).

Azure CLI is a native cross-platform command-line tool that allows us to manage Azure (like Azure PowerShell).

Installing Azure CLI can be done using the following methods:

- Installer file

- PowerShell (download and install)

- Windows Package Manager (WinGet)

- Zip package

Based on the use case of this book, I recommend you install Azure CLI using WinGet. The following WinGet command will install the latest version of Azure CLI on a Windows machine.

```
winget install -e --id Microsoft.AzureCLI
```

If you are on a Windows machine, I recommend you enable Tab Completion in PowerShell using these steps.

Note   On a non-Windows operating system, the following step is not required, as tab completion is enabled by default.

Enable Azure CLI Tab Completion (Windows Only)

The following commands and code will create a PowerShell profile, which will load a PowerShell script that will enable Tab Completion for the Azure CLI command line.

Create a PowerShell Profile

On a Windows machine, open PowerShell as Administrator and run the following command:

```
if (!(Test-Path -Path $PROFILE)) {
  New-Item -ItemType File -Path $PROFILE -Force
}
```

Open the profile file using the following command:

```
Notepad $PROFILE
```

Copy the following code to the file. Save the file and restart PowerShell.

```
Register-ArgumentCompleter -Native -CommandName az
-ScriptBlock {
    param($commandName, $wordToComplete, $cursorPosition)
    $completion_file = New-TemporaryFile
```

```
$env:ARGCOMPLETE_USE_TEMPFILES = 1
$env:_ARGCOMPLETE_STDOUT_FILENAME = $completion_file
$env:COMP_LINE = $wordToComplete
$env:COMP_POINT = $cursorPosition
$env:_ARGCOMPLETE = 1
$env:_ARGCOMPLETE_SUPPRESS_SPACE = 0
$env:_ARGCOMPLETE_IFS = "`n"
$env:_ARGCOMPLETE_SHELL = 'powershell'
az 2>&1 | Out-Null
Get-Content $completion_file | Sort-Object |
ForEach-Object {
    [System.Management.Automation.
    CompletionResult]::new($_, $_, "ParameterValue", $_)
}
Remove-Item $completion_file, Env:\_ARGCOMPLETE_STDOUT_
FILENAME, Env:\ARGCOMPLETE_USE_TEMPFILES, Env:\COMP_LINE,
Env:\COMP_POINT, Env:\_ARGCOMPLETE, Env:\_ARGCOMPLETE_
SUPPRESS_SPACE, Env:\_ARGCOMPLETE_IFS, Env:\_
ARGCOMPLETE_SHELL
}
```

Next time when using Azure CLI, use the tab key on the keyboard to complete commands.

Azure Cloud Shell

Before we move to the next section, I would like to offer the option to use Azure Cloud Shell to run Azure PowerShell or Azure CLI commands.

Azure Cloud Shell is an Azure service that offers an integrated terminal in the browser that can run Azure PowerShell or Azure CLI. In addition to these two tools, Azure Cloud Shell comes preloaded with many cloud management tools (including Microsoft 365) and development tools like databases and programming languages.

The following list shows all the tools that are available on Cloud Shell:

- Docker Desktop
- Kubectl
- Helm
- D2iQ Kubernetes Platform CLI
- Cloud Foundry CLI
- Terraform
- Ansible
- Chef InSpec
- Puppet Bolt
- HashiCorp Packer
- make
- maven
- npm
- pip
- Git
- GitHub CLI
- MySQL client
- PostgreSql client
- sqlcmd Utility

- mssql-scripter

- .NET Core 7.0

- PowerShell 7.4

- Node.js

- Java

- Python 3.9

- Ruby

- Go

- bash

- zsh

- sh

- tmux

- dig

- Office 365 CLI

- Azure CLI

- Azure PowerShell

- Az.Tools.Predictor

- AzCopy

- Azure Functions CLI

- Service Fabric CLI

- Batch Shipyard

- blobxfer

- Exchange Online PowerShell

- A basic set of Microsoft Graph PowerShell modules

- Microsoft.Graph.Applications

- Microsoft.Graph.Authentication

- Microsoft.Graph.Groups

- Microsoft.Graph.Identity.DirectoryManagement

- Microsoft.Graph.Identity.Governance

- Microsoft.Graph.Identity.SignIns

- Microsoft.Graph.Users.Actions

- Microsoft.Graph.Users.Functions

- MicrosoftPowerBIMgmt PowerShell modules

- SqlServer PowerShell modules

Behind the scenes, Azure Cloud Shell runs a Linux image and uses an Azure storage account to save changes made to the image.

The cost of using Azure Cloud Shell is based on storing the image as blob storage in Azure. Azure does not charge for running the image as a compute service.

Use Azure Cloud Shell

To get started with Azure Cloud Shell, login to the Azure portal and click the Azure Cloud Shell icon, as shown in Figure 2-15.

Figure 2-15. *Start Azure Cloud Shell*

If Cloud Shell is not configured on your subscription, you will be asked to set up a storage account or use an ephemeral session that will not save the state of your work.

Figure 2-16 shows the Azure Cloud Shell drop-down menu that allows you to switch from Azure CLI to Azure PowerShell.

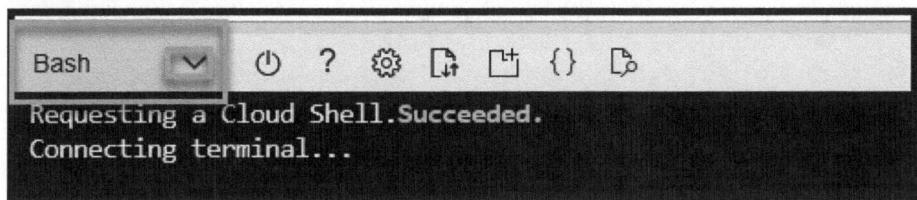

Figure 2-16. *Azure Cloud Shell drop-down menu*

Use Azure Cloud Shell with VS Code

If you like VS Code's look and feel and would still like to use Azure Cloud Shell and do not worry about installing and maintaining Azure CLI, PowerShell, and your development tools for Azure work, you can access Azure Cloud Shell directly from VS Code.

To use Azure Cloud Shell, we first need to install Node.js.

Go to Node.js website `https://nodejs.org/en/download/current` and download the latest version, as shown in Figure 2-17.

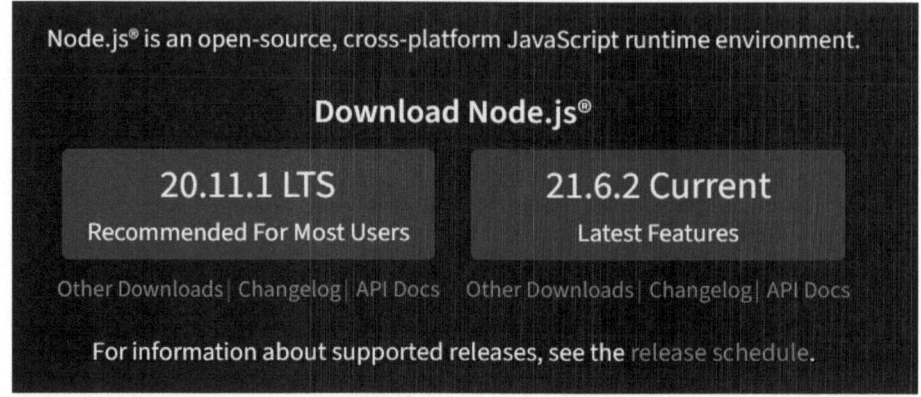

Figure 2-17. *Download Node.js*

Install the Azure Account VS Code extension (if not already installed) as shown in Figure 2-18.

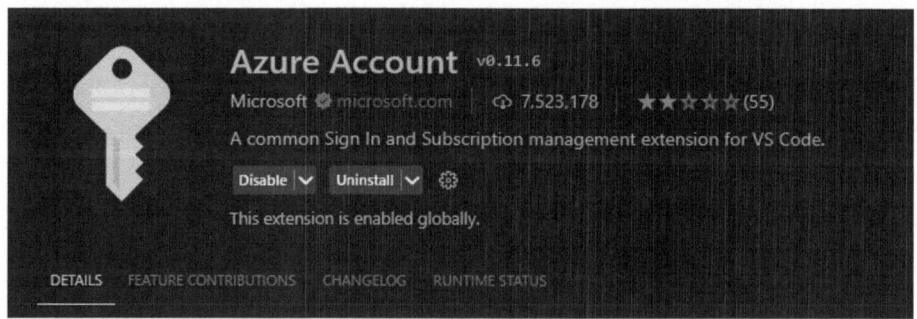

Figure 2-18. *Azure Account*

In the context of Cloud Shell, the Azure Account extension allows us to sign in to Azure and manage the subscription.

Open VS Code.

Click View ➤ Command Palette

In the Command Palette text box, type Azure Sign in, as shown in Figure 2-19.

Figure 2-19. *Azure Sign In*

After authenticating to Azure, return to VS Code and open the terminal windows.

Click the add terminal window from the terminal window and select Azure Cloud Shell (PowerShell) or Azure Cloud Shell (Bash).

Figure 2-20 shows the terminal window with the Cloud Shell options.

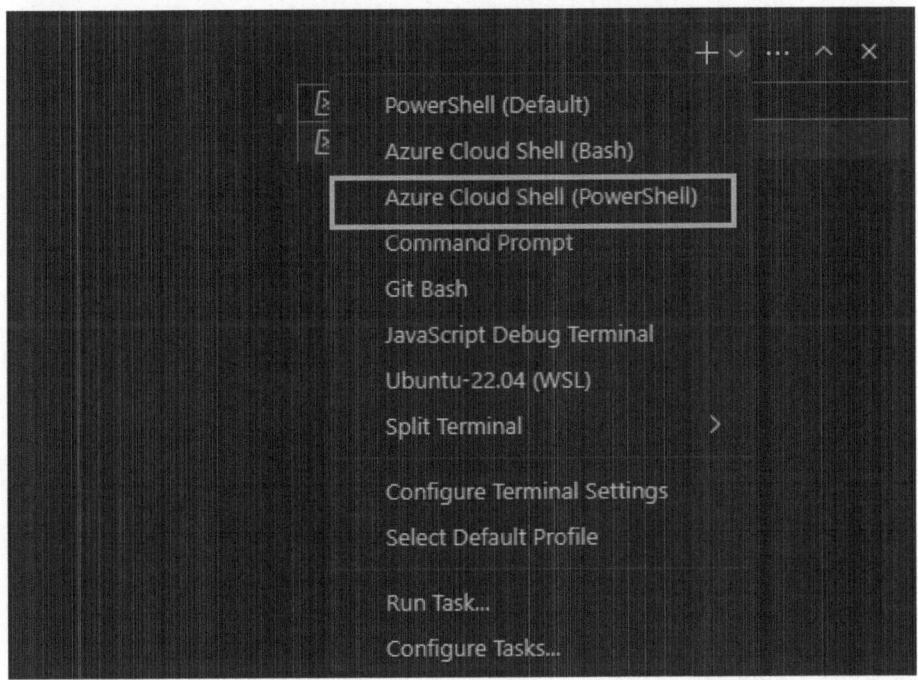

Figure 2-20. *Azure Cloud Shell (VS Code)*

Using Cloud Shell has several benefits, which include always up-to-date tools, and it also offers a secure environment located in Azure.

You might not find Azure Cloud Shell suitable for your development needs; however, it is an option that can accommodate several use cases.

Install Terraform

Another great tool that allows us to deploy and manage Azure resources (infrastructure) programmatically is Terraform.

Terraform is the most popular and widely used infrastructure as code (IaC) software development tool available on the market and is considered an industry standard for infrastructure deployment.

It is also the most mature tool for infrastructure deployments and has been around for many years. Terraform supports most major cloud providers, like AWS and GCP.

Terraform uses the concept of domain-specific language (DSL), also known as HashiCorp Configuration Language (HCL). The idea behind the language is to use a declarative approach to infrastructure code.

In the declarative approach, we define the desired state of the infrastructure and let Terraform handle the deployment and configuration.

High-Level Example of Terraform

The following code, for example, creates an Azure Resource Group using Terraform:

```
# main.tf
provider "azurerm" {
  features {}
}

resource "azurerm_resource_group" "example" {
```

```
name     = "Apress-ch01"
location = "West Europe"
}
```

The preceding example has a Terraform configuration file called main.tf.

It is important to note that all Terraform configuration files need to use the .TF file extension for Terraform to deploy them.

The following code declares that we are using the Microsoft Azure Terraform provider.

In Terraform, a provider has all the domain-specific code to deploy resources to a cloud provider like Azure. Each cloud provider has its own Terraform provider.

The Azure Terraform provider is called azurerm.

```
provider "azurerm" {
  features {}
}
```

Next, we tell Terraform to create a resource group in Azure Web Europe datacenter. The name of the resource group is Apress-ch01.

Once we run the code, Terraform will deploy the resource group.

We will review the process to set up and deploy a resource soon. The above code is just a high-level example of how Terraform deploys infrastructure.

Install

Now that we have seen and learned a bit about Terraform, let's talk about the installation process of Terraform.

Terraform is available on Linux, macOS, and Windows. My recommendation in this book is that you use Terraform on WSL, macOS, or Linux. Because many DevOps tools are available natively on Linux and macOS, using Windows doesn't produce the best development results.

63

Install Terraform on macOS

The recommended method to install Terraform on macOS is using a package manager, and in our case, it is best to use Brew.

To install Terraform using Brew, use the following commands from your macOS terminal.

First, install the Hashicorp repository using the following tap command:

```
brew tap hashicorp/tap
```

To install Terraform, run the following command:

```
brew install hashicorp/tap/terraform
```

If you already have Terraform installed and want to update it to the latest version, use the following command:

First, update Brew using the update command:

```
brew update
```

Once Brew is updated, run the following command:

```
brew upgrade hashicorp/tap/terraform
```

At this stage, Terraform is ready. To check which version of Terraform is installed on your machine, run the following:

```
terraform -version
```

Enable Terraform Tab Completion

To enable tab completion for Terraform, first, make sure you have the Bash profile configured by running the following command:

```
Touch ~/bashrc
```

Then, run the following command:

```
terraform -install-autocomplete
```

Install Terraform on Linux

In this section, I'm going to install Terraform on Ubuntu only; however, if you run a different Linux distribution, please refer to the following URL:

https://developer.hashicorp.com/terraform/tutorials/aws-get-started/install-cli

Terraform is available on the following Linux distributions:

- CentOS/RHEL

- Fedora

- Amazon Linux

Install Terraform on Ubuntu Linux

To install Terraform on Ubuntu, we first need to install the HashiCorp package repository:

```
wget -O- https://apt.releases.hashicorp.com/gpg | sudo gpg
--dearmor -o /usr/share/keyrings/hashicorp-archive-keyring.gpg
```

Then, we need to install the GPG security signature using the following command:

```
echo "deb [signed-by=/usr/share/keyrings/hashicorp-archive-
keyring.gpg] https://apt.releases.hashicorp.com $(lsb_release
-cs) main" | sudo tee /etc/apt/sources.list.d/hashicorp.list
```

The last command will install Terraform.

```
sudo apt update && sudo apt install terraform
```

Enable Terraform Tab Completion on Ubuntu

To enable tab completion for Terraform on Linux Ubuntu, first, make sure you have the Bash profile configured by running the following command:

```
Touch ~/bashrc
```

Then, run the following command:

```
terraform -install-autocomplete
```

Install Terraform on Windows

The recommended method to install Terraform on Windows is using a package manager, and for Windows, we are going to use Winget again to install Terraform.

To search for Terraform with Winget, open a PowerShell terminal and run the following command:

```
winget search terraform
```

The output from the command is shown below. The current version is 1.5.3.

To install Terraform, run the following command:

```
Winget install Hashicorp.Terraform
```

Note   Parts of the Install Terraform section were copied from my second edition books about Terraform and Azure, *Getting Started with Containers in Azure* and *Deploy Secure Cloud Applications Using Terraform.*

Install Postman

Another tool that I would like to recommend is Postman. Postman is a popular tool for testing and developing APIs.

It allows us to do the following tasks:

- Send API requests (POST, PUT, etc.).

- Manage responses from an API endpoint.

- Debug API issues using an intuitive user interface.

We can also use Postman to create and run automated tests, document APIs, and collaborate with other developers.

Postman supports major formats and protocols, such as REST, GraphQL, SOAP, and gRPC.

In the context of Azure OpenAI, we can use the Postman client (Web or desktop) to connect to an Azure OpenAI endpoint and send requests to a model.

This is handy for testing an API feature or running an operation.

To download and install Postman, go to the following URL `www.postman.com/downloads/` as shown in Figure 2-21 and download the version suitable for your operating system.

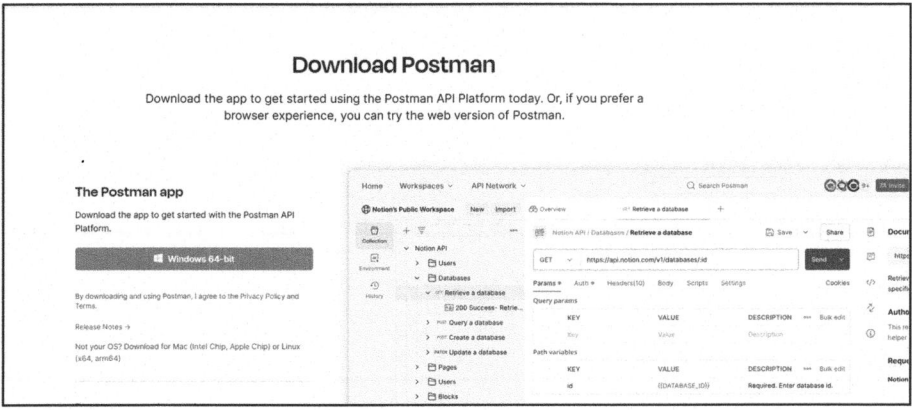

Figure 2-21. *Install Postman*

Postman also comes in a Web version.

To use the Postman web version, create a free Postman account and login to Postman using the following URL `www.postman.com/`.

Click on Workspaces.

Click on My Workspace.

As shown in Figure 2-22, I am using Postman web to connect to a GPT4 model in Azure OpenAI using REST API.

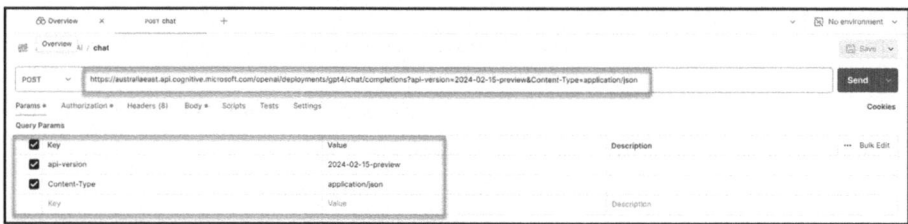

Figure 2-22. *Postman web interface*

In the request, I'm using the following:

- API Operation – POST

- Endpoint – Chat

- Params – Passing API version and content type

In Figure 2-23, you can see the entire endpoint URL and that it is made of two parameters.

- Api-version

- Content-type

Figure 2-23. *POST request to Azure OpenAI endpoint*

In Figure 2-24, you can see the parameters I'm passing the endpoint.

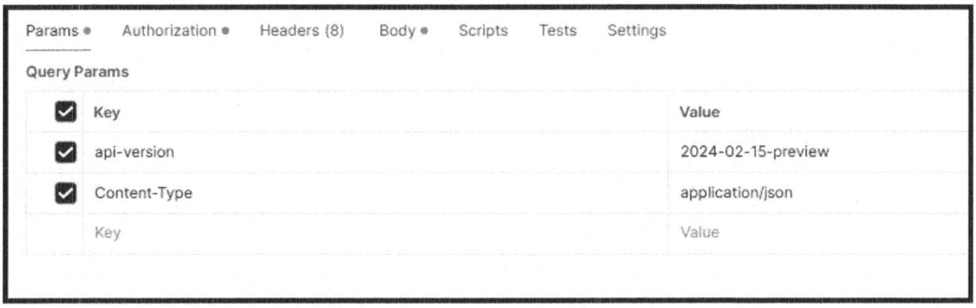

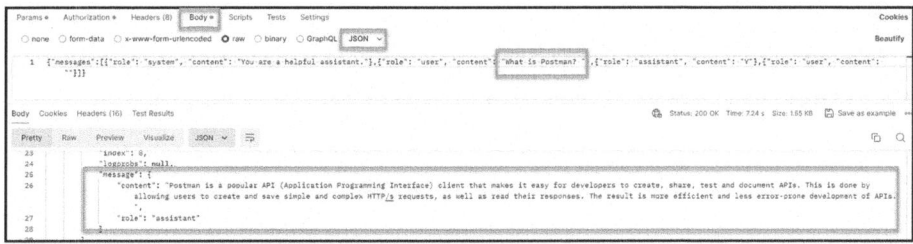

Figure 2-24. Query Params

In Figure 2-25, you can see how I use Postman to send a prompt to Azure OpenAI.

Figure 2-25. Postman in use

I'm using the Body section (JSON format) to format my prompt and ask What is Postman?

In the lower section, you can see the reply from the model.

Later in the book, we will use Postman to issue API requests to an Azure OpenAI endpoint and go through the steps needed to communicate with an Azure OpenAI endpoint successfully.

Install Git

Git is the world's most popular source code management tool that allows us to collaborate and manage code. With git, we can create snapshots of our code using commits and work with different versions of it.

We use a branch to create a new version of our code and add changes to it and when completed commit it to online platforms like GitHub or Azure DevOps where we can store it and create pipelines that build applications or infrastructure.

Git is free and open source and runs on all major operating systems. To install Git on Windows, we can use the WinGet package manager using the following command:

```
Winget install Git.Git
```

We can also use the GUI installation method by going to the following URL https://git-scm.com/download/win as shown in Figure 2-26.

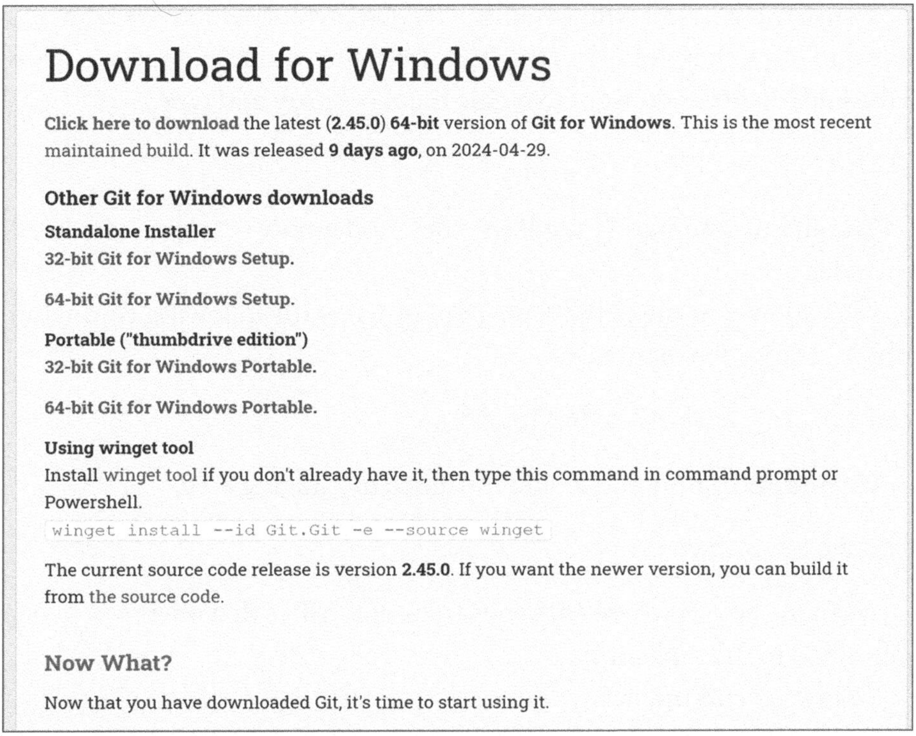

Download for Windows

Click here to download the latest (**2.45.0**) **64-bit** version of **Git for Windows**. This is the most recent maintained build. It was released **9 days ago**, on 2024-04-29.

Other Git for Windows downloads

Standalone Installer
32-bit Git for Windows Setup.

64-bit Git for Windows Setup.

Portable ("thumbdrive edition")
32-bit Git for Windows Portable.

64-bit Git for Windows Portable.

Using winget tool
Install winget tool if you don't already have it, then type this command in command prompt or Powershell.

```
winget install --id Git.Git -e --source winget
```

The current source code release is version **2.45.0**. If you want the newer version, you can build it from the source code.

Now What?

Now that you have downloaded Git, it's time to start using it.

Figure 2-26. *Download Git*

How to Use Git

After downloading the Git installer and installing Git, use the following steps to get started with Git. These steps are very basic but will help you get started with Git if you're new to it.

Start with opening PowerShell or a Shell terminal and run the following command to check the installed version:

```
git --version
```

The output will show the version of Git installed on the machine.

71

To use Git, we start with creating a local repository where we store our code and track changes to it. To do this, from the command line, navigate to the folder where you want to create the repository and type:

```
git init
```

The git init command initializes a new and empty Git repository inside the folder.

Let's add a new file to the repository by using the following command or by creating a file manually:

```
echo "Hello, world!" > hello.txt
```

Use the add command to add the file to the staging area.

```
git add hello.txt
```

A staging area is where Git keeps track of the files that are ready to be committed to the repository.

To make a commit, we type:

```
git commit -m "Initial commit"
```

This will save the file to the repository with the message "Initial commit."

We can use the git status command to see the state of our repository. The state can be

- Staged

- Untracked

We can use the git log command to see the history of our commits which include

- Author

- Date

- Message of each commit

You can use the git diff command to see the changes made to the files in your repository.

GitHub Copilot

As an optional feature, I would like to talk about GiHub Copilot and go through the installation process of the service.

GitHub Copilot is an AI assistant that is based on OpenAI models and helps us write code in many programming languages. The core competency of the product is Python, C#, and many other languages.

GitHub Copilot is not free and does not come in a free tier offer. Currently, GitHub offers three price tiers as shown in Figure 2-27.

Figure 2-27. *GitHub Copilot pricing*

The most popular tier is the Business tier, as shown in Figure 2-27a, which offers most of the AI capabilities needed for software development for an SMB business or consultants.

Figure 2-27a shows the feature set of each tier.

Figure 2-27a. *GitHub Copilot feature set of each tier*

If you go with the business tier, you will have to configure your GitHub account with an organization so you can assign licenses to yourself or other people that are working with you.

After setting up your GitHub organization, you need to assign a GitHub Copilot license to yourself or others working with you in the same GitHub organization.

The license will be activated automatically when they log into GitHub from VS Code or Visual Studio. To use GitHub Copilot in VS Code, Install the GitHub Copilot extension as shown in Figure 2-28.

Figure 2-28. *GitHub Copilot extension*

After finishing the installation, click the Sign in to GitHub button from the pop-up window in VS Code, as shown in Figure 2-29.

Figure 2-29. *Sign in to GitHub Copilot*

After signing in, you can access GitHub Copilot from VS Code using the GitHub Copilot icon at the bottom right corner, shown in Figure 2-30.

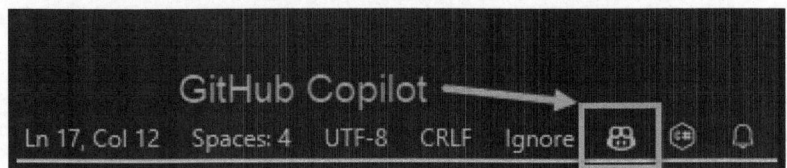

Figure 2-30. *GitHub Copilot*

How to Use GitHub Copilot

Using GitHub Copilot is straightforward, and we do so using the keyboard shortcuts. The following table shows the keyboard shortcuts for using GitHub Copilot.

Action	Shortcut
Accept an inline code suggestion	Tab
Dismiss an inline code suggestion	Esc
Show next inline code suggestion	Alt+]
Show previous inline code suggestion	Alt+[
Trigger inline code suggestion	Alt+\
Open GitHub Copilot suggestions in separate pane	Alt+Enter

To get the best of GitHub Copilot, we first need to create a file with an extension corresponding to a programming language and open the file with the VS Code editor. In Figure 2-31, I have a C# file with a .CS extension.

Copilot shows the suggestion inline prompt when I open the file to help us get started.

Note   Depending on your VS Code configuration, you might have different keyboard shortcuts (as shown in Figure 2-31).

Figure 2-31. *GitHub copilot prompt*

We can also access Copilot from the Chat menu and ask questions regarding specific files, sections, and editors using the # key. If you type /, Copilot will offer common suggestions like /fix (fixing and issue and more).

Figure 2-32 shows the GitHub CoPilot.

Figure 2-32. *GitHub Copilot Chat icon*

You can ask the Copilot open-form questions or specific questions about files, sections, and more from the chat menu. If you type / in the chat menu, you will see predefined help and suggestions Copilot has (Figure 2-33).

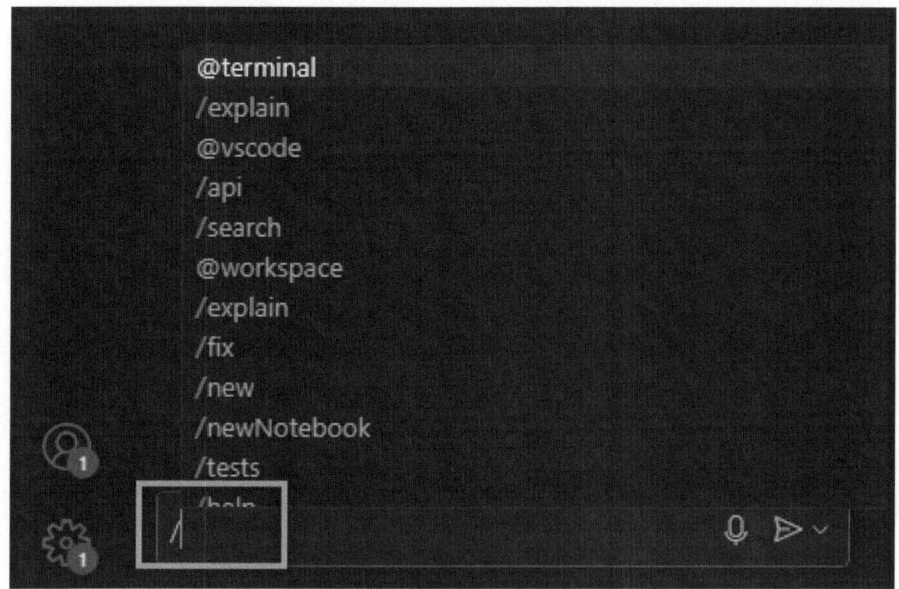

Figure 2-33. *GitHub Copilot Chat terminal*

To ask the Copilot specific questions about your code, use the #editor and ask a question.

Chapter Summary

This chapter focuses on the tools needed to develop Azure OpenAI solutions. The main goal of this chapter is to introduce you to enough tools to make your life easier.

In the next chapter, we will create our first Azure OpenAI resource and will create a C# program that uses the service.

CHAPTER 3

Azure .NET SDK for Azure OpenAI and AI Services

Introduction

This chapter will begin a practical and technical journey of building a chat application with C# and the Azure SDK for .NET.

To create an AI application, we must deploy an Azure OpenAI resource and deploy a model (GPT4 or GPT3.5). We will use many of the tools we installed in Chapter 2 in this chapter.

The Azure OpenAI resource and model deployment components are the crucial backbone of any AI application on Microsoft Azure. Understanding their importance is critical to learning Azure OpenAI and Azure because we need a Microsoft Azure infrastructure and resources to run or use Azure OpenAI.

In this chapter, we will use the following tools to deploy and access Azure OpenAI resources and model:

- Azure Portal

- Azure CLI

© The Editor(s) (if applicable) and The Author(s),
under exclusive license to APress Media, LLC, part of Springer Nature 2024
S. Ifrah, *Getting Started with Azure OpenAI*, https://doi.org/10.1007/979-8-8688-0599-8_3

- Azure PowerShell

- Postman

- C#

Figure 3-1 shows how resource deployment, application, and Azure are connected.

In this book, we will follow the following process:

1. Create a Microsoft Azure OpenAI resource – This is the infrastructure part of our application, and we can create the OpenAI resource using the Azure Portal, PowerShell, Azure CLI, or Terraform.

2. Create a C# application – Using the Azure SDK for .NET, we create a .NET application that consumes and uses the Azure OpenAI resource.

To help you understand the process, I created the diagram in Figure 3-1 and clarified the connection between all the components that make an AI application on Azure.

An application can also consume and use other Azure infrastructure resources like storage, computing, web services, and more.

In our initial example, our application will run on a local machine, but later on we will host an application on Azure.

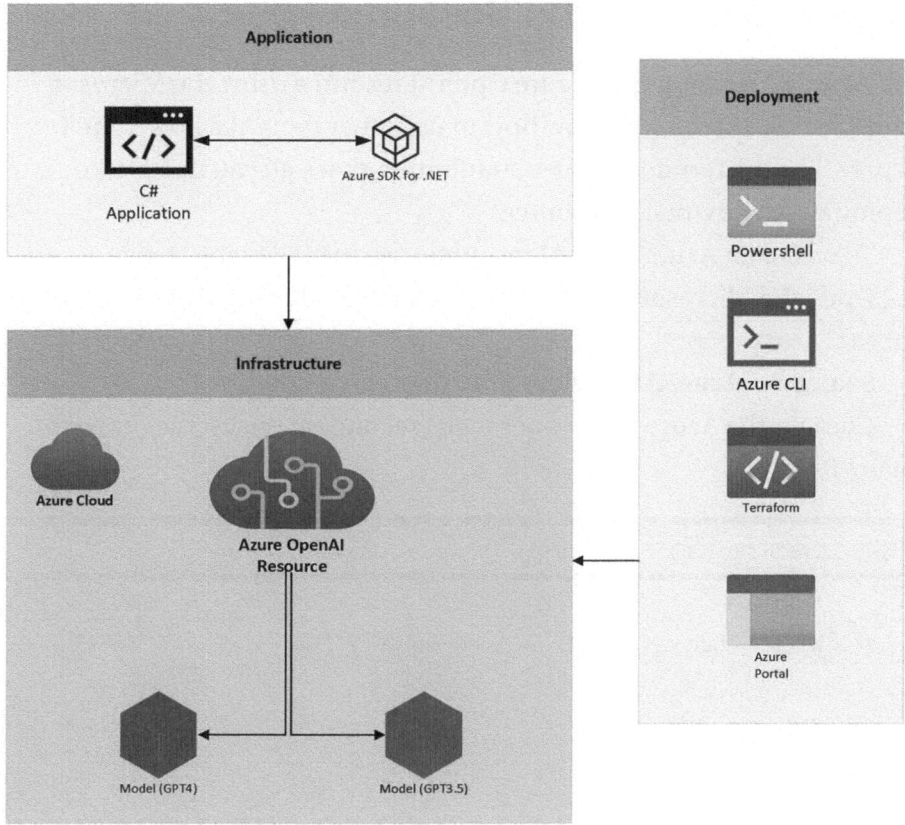

Figure 3-1. *Azure OpenAI*

At minimum to get started with Azure OpenAI, all we need is an OpenAI resource and a single deployment of a model. If you remember from Chapter 1, a model can be a GPT4 or GPT3.5 model. To use Azure OpenAI, we need an OpenAI resource and a model.

An OpenAI resource can host multiple models and is only limited to the subscription tenant, as we discussed in Chapter 1.

Deploy Azure OpenAI Resource

Let's start with creating an Azure OpenAI resource using the Microsoft Azure portal. Later, I will show how to use other tools like PowerShell, Azure CLI, and Terraform, but at minimum, that's all you need to know to deploy an Azure OpenAI resource.

To create an Azure OpenAI resource, use the following steps.

Open the Microsoft Azure portal using the following URL: `https://portal.azure.com`

Search for Azure AI Services from the search box.

Click on the Azure AI Services icon (second on the list) as shown in Figure 3-2.

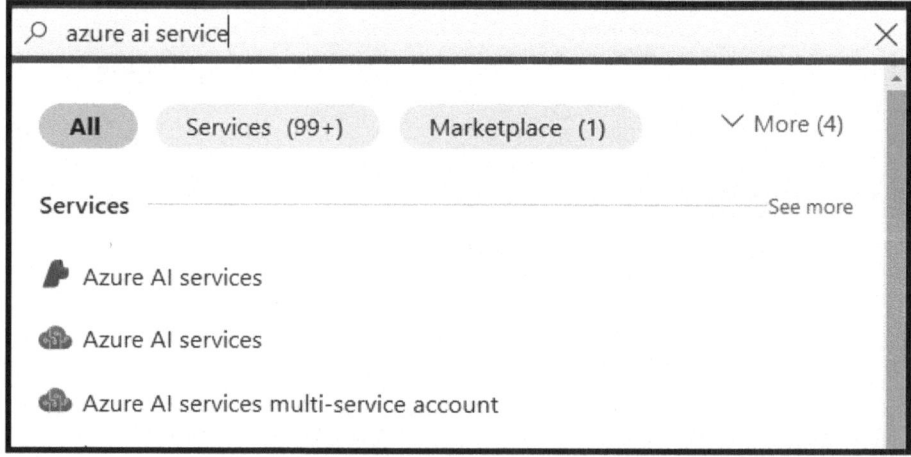

Figure 3-2. *Azure AI Services*

From the AI Services page, click on the Create under Azure OpenAI account as shown in Figure 3-3.

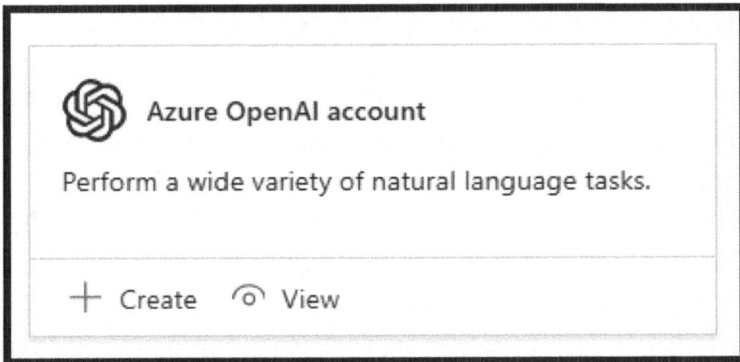

Figure 3-3. *Azure OpenAI account*

In the Create Azure OpenAI account page, use the following settings.

Subscription	Select Your Subscription
Resource group	Create a new resource group with the name rg-apress
Region	Select a region
Name	Name your resources with the name: oai-apress
Pricing tier	S0

Click next and select All Networks in the Network section.

Click Create to deploy the Azure OpenAI resource, and wait for the resource to be ready.

Note   If you would like to follow Microsoft Azure abbreviations recommendations for naming Azure resources, please visit the following page: `https://learn.microsoft.com/en-us/azure/cloud-adoption-framework/ready/azure-best-practices/resource-abbreviations`

Get Endpoint and API Key Information

To access an Azure OpenAI service, we need three pieces of information: API Key, Endpoint URL, and deployment name. We will start with retrieving the first two (API Key and Endpoint URL).

From the Azure portal, open the Azure OpenAI resource by clicking Azure AI Services.

Under Azure OpenAI account, click on **View**.

From the Azure OpenAI page, click on Keys and Endpoint, as shown in Figure 3-4.

Copy KEY 1 and the Endpoint URL.

Note   Keep the KEY 1 information in a secure location and never commit it to a Git repository.

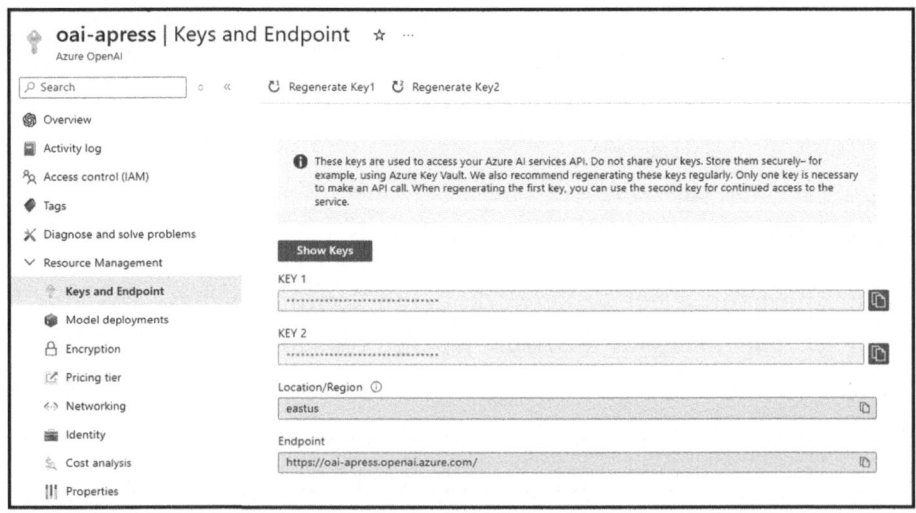

Figure 3-4. *Keys and Endpoint*

Deploy a Model

The next step is to deploy a model from the Azure AI portal.

To deploy a model from the Azure portal, click the newly created OpenAI resource, and from the top menu, click Go to Azure OpenAI Studio, as shown in Figure 3-5.

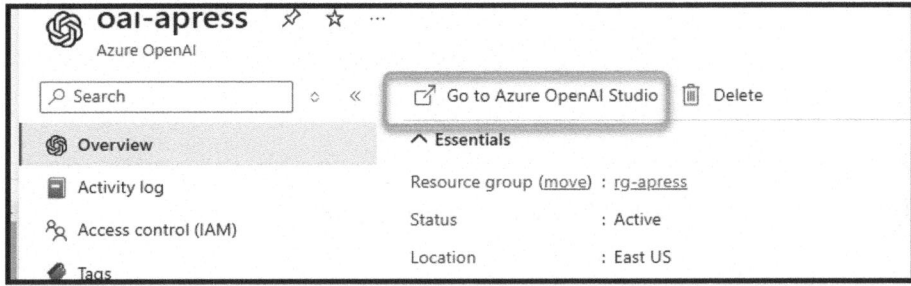

Figure 3-5. *Azure OpenAI Studio*

Note   To create and manage Azure OpenAI Deployments, Microsoft made a dedicated portal for OpenAI (`https://oai.azure.com/portal`).

The Azure OpenAI Studio gives us several tools that allow us to develop an AI application, and once the functionality of the app is ready, program it using an SDK or REST API.

The left menu gives us access to playgrounds to test deployed models, as shown in Figure 3-6.

Note   To switch between deployments, use the top right menu. Click the deployment name, and under the Current resource, click Switch.

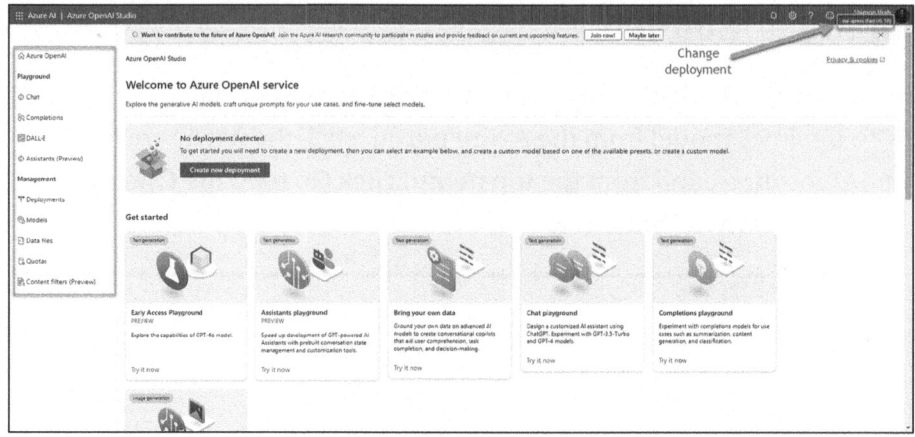

Figure 3-6. *Azure OpenAI Studio home page*

To deploy an OpenAI model, Click **Deployments**.

From the Deployments page, Click **Create new deployment**.

Use the following details on the Deploy model page, as shown in Figure 3-7.

Select a model	Gpt-4
Model version	Auto-update to default
Deployment type	Standard
Deployment name	Gpt-4
Enable Dynamic Quota	Enabled

Note   It is highly recommended to name the deployment (Deployment name) using the same name as the selected model.

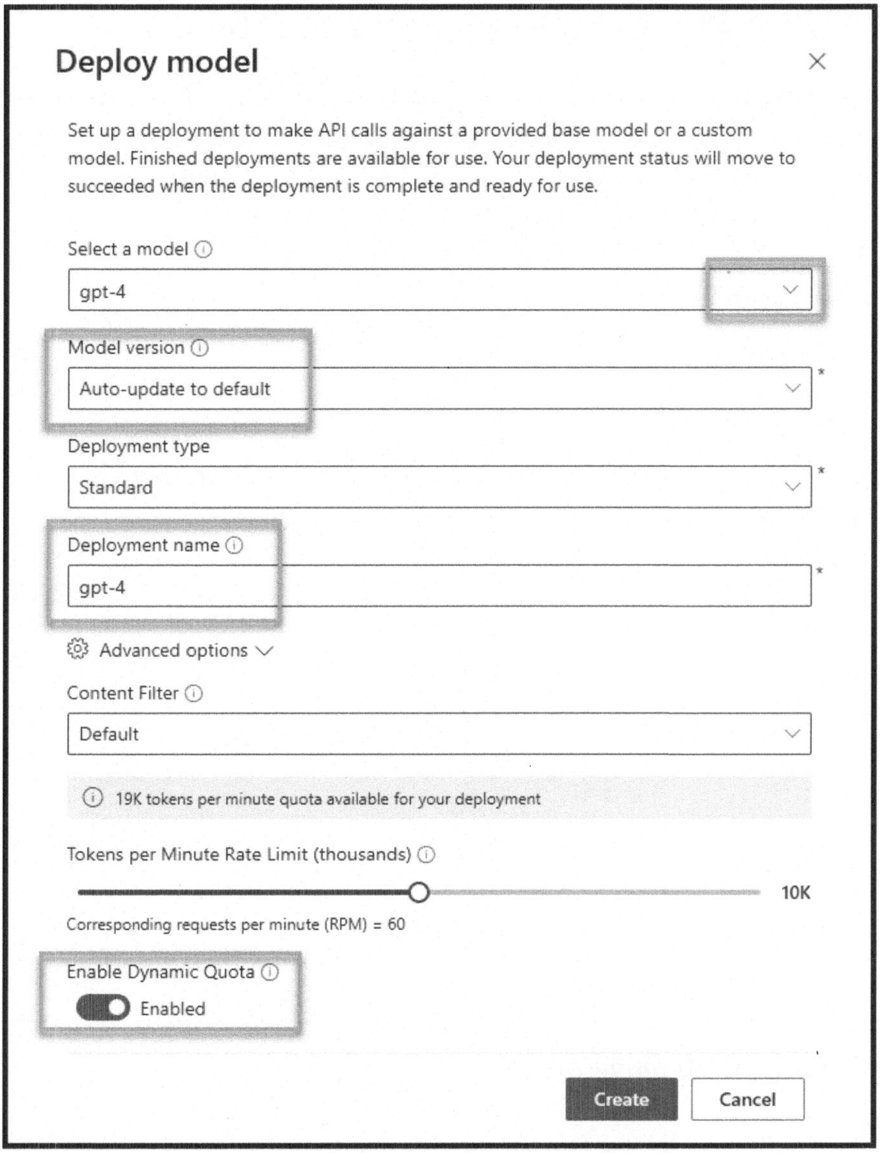

Figure 3-7. *Deploy an Azure OpenAI model*

Once the model is deployed, you will see it on the Deployment page.

Use Chat Playground to Test the Model

Now that we have an Azure OpenAI resource and model, it is time to test them. Azure makes it easier for us to test models by using Playgrounds.

Currently, the OpenAI Studio offers us the following Playgrounds:

- Chat

- Completions

- DALL-E

- Assistant (Preview)

To try the chat playground. Click on Chat under Playground in the OpenAI portal, as shown in the Figure 3-8.

Figure 3-8. *Chat playground*

To test the model, we can use predefined templates and configure the deployment parameters (available from the Configuration menu, Parameters tab).

In Figure 3-9, I'm using the JSON formatter assistant template that uses natural language to create JSON format files. In the example, I'm asking the model (gpt-4) to create a JSON file that I will use with an ARM template to create a Windows Virtual Machine on Azure.

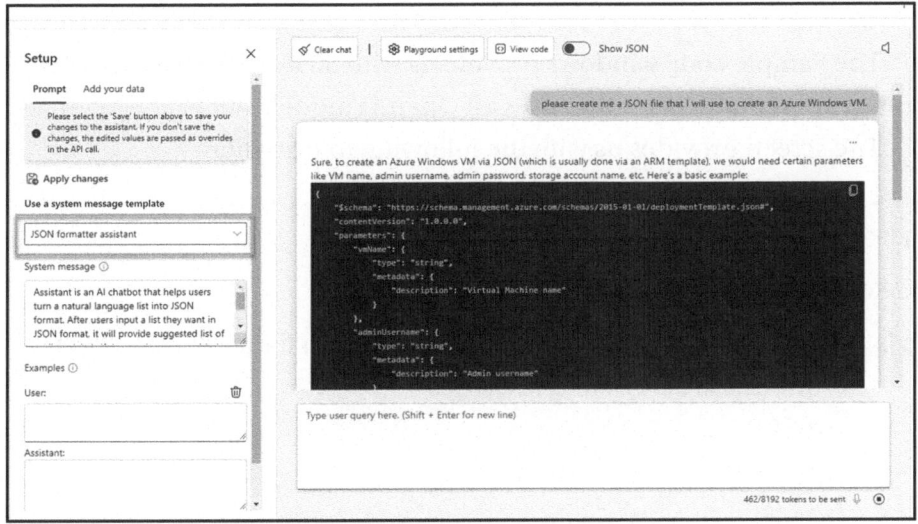

Figure 3-9. *JSON formatter assistant template*

View Code and Endpoint Details

Once I'm happy with the results and ready to deploy the model into the application, Azure gives us two options:

- Provide us with the deployment code, endpoint, and key.

- Deploy directly to an Azure Web App.

Let's begin with the first option. To view the deployment code from the Chat playground window, click on the View code button, as shown in Figure 3-10.

Figure 3-10. *View code*

The Sample code windows provide us with all the information we need to start an AI application that uses an OpenAI model.

The screen provides us with the following information.

Endpoint This is the OpenAI resource endpoint URL.

API Key   Security key to access the endpoint

Code   The code section shows the integration code of the application, which is available in the following languages:
- C#
- Python
- Curl

Figure 3-11 shows the View code screen.

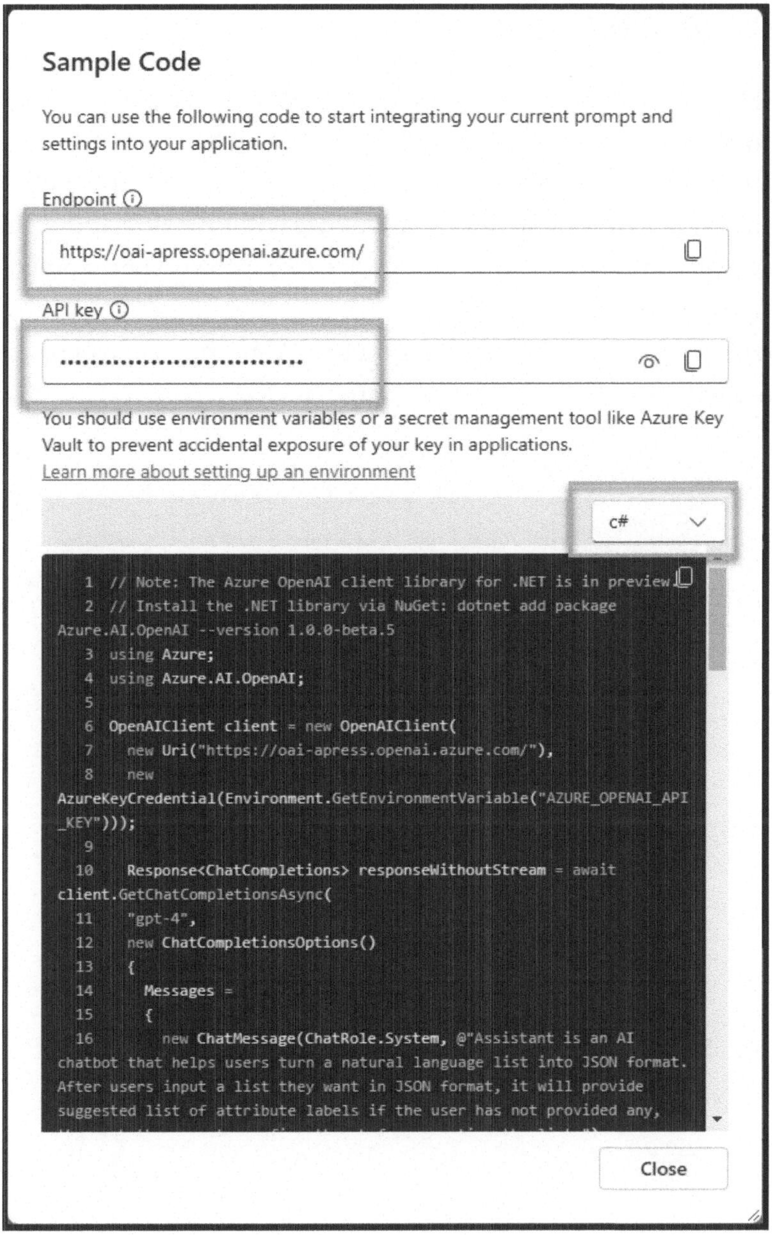

Sample Code

You can use the following code to start integrating your current prompt and settings into your application.

Endpoint ⓘ

```
https://oai-apress.openai.azure.com/                                    ▢
```

API key ⓘ

```
.................................                                  ◌   ▢
```

You should use environment variables or a secret management tool like Azure Key Vault to prevent accidental exposure of your key in applications.
Learn more about setting up an environment

```                                                                 c#   ⌄

  1  // Note: The Azure OpenAI client library for .NET is in preview ▢
  2  // Install the .NET library via NuGet: dotnet add package
Azure.AI.OpenAI --version 1.0.0-beta.5
  3  using Azure;
  4  using Azure.AI.OpenAI;
  5
  6  OpenAIClient client = new OpenAIClient(
  7     new Uri("https://oai-apress.openai.azure.com/"),
  8     new
AzureKeyCredential(Environment.GetEnvironmentVariable("AZURE_OPENAI_API
_KEY")));
  9
 10     Response<ChatCompletions> responseWithoutStream = await
client.GetChatCompletionsAsync(
 11     "gpt-4",
 12     new ChatCompletionsOptions()
 13     {
 14       Messages =
 15       {
 16         new ChatMessage(ChatRole.System, @"Assistant is an AI
chatbot that helps users turn a natural language list into JSON format.
After users input a list they want in JSON format, it will provide
suggested list of attribute labels if the user has not provided any,
```

                                                                    Close

Figure 3-11. *Sample Code*

Deploy to Web App

Clicking the Deploy To button shown in Figure 3-8 will give you the option to deploy your chat application to an Azure Web App.

Azure Web Apps is a service that allows us to run web applications written in .NET, Python, and other languages without worrying about the underlying infrastructure of the service like web servers, storage, web configurations, and more.

When you deploy a chat application to a Web App, you will be presented with the screen shown in Figure 3-11a.

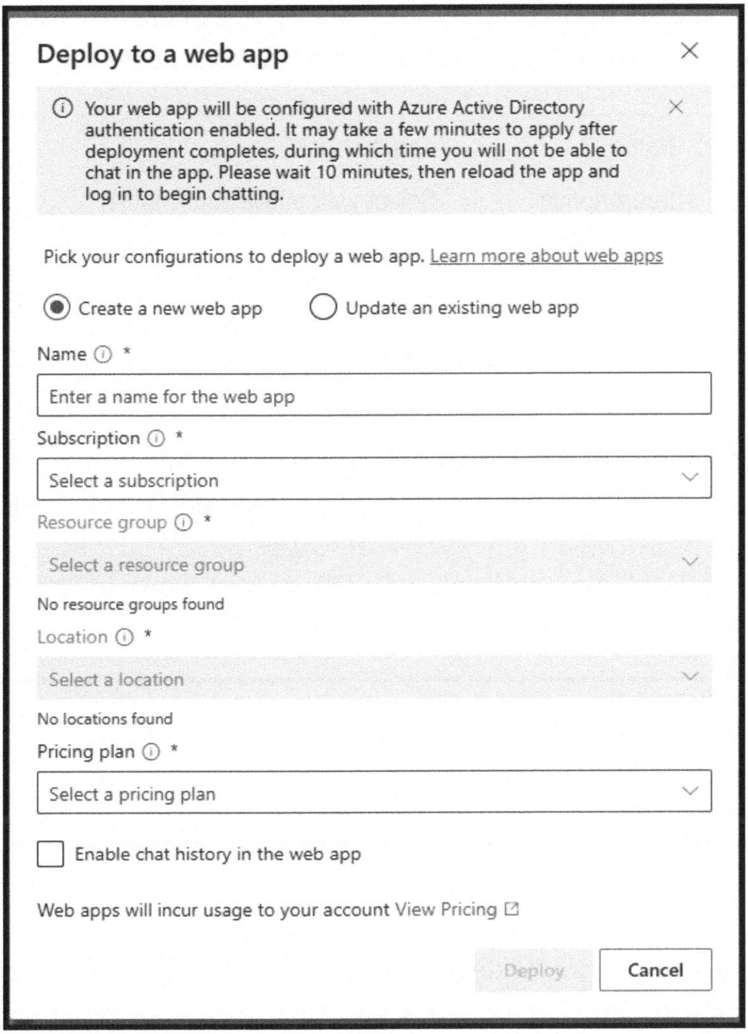

Figure 3-11a. *Deploy to a web app*

Azure will ask us to either create a new service or use an existing one. Select Create a new web App and fill in the following details.

Name	app-apress
Subscription	Select your active subscription
Resource group	rg-apress-app
Pricing plan	B1
Enable chat history	Yes

Click deploy and wait for the web app to be ready.

You can access the web app from the Azure portal by searching for App Services and clicking the app-apress Web App.

From the Web App main page, click Browse, as shown in Figure 3-11b, to see the chat application in a web format.

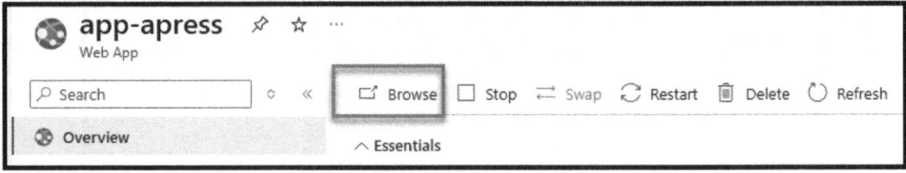

Figure 3-11b. *Browse Web App*

Figure 3-11c shows the deployed chat application. By default, it comes with a Contoso logo, which can be customized with a different brand.

By default, the app is deployed with Entra ID authentication, so you will need to use your Azure credentials to log in before using the app.

Upgrade the Web App Service Plan if the application takes too long to load.

Figure 3-11c. *Deployed chat application*

Create a C# Console Application

We are ready to create a C# Console app using an Azure OpenAI GPT model. At this stage, we have everything we need to create an application, and we will create a C# application that generates a secure password and counts the tokens the request used.

We can use Visual Studio Code or Visual Studio to create our first application.

Let's start with creating a C# console application. From the VS Code terminal window, run the following commands.

We start with creating a directory that will host the application:

```
mkdir aoi-ch3-app
```

Create a C# application (by default, the application name will be the same as the directory name, and it will use the latest .NET version that is installed on the machine. In our case, it will be .NET 8). If you need to use a different name and .NET target version, use the –name and –framework switches:

```
dotnet new console
```

Adds Tokenizer Configuration Files

As I explained, we are creating a C# console application that generates a secure password and counts the number of tokens the request uses. To count token, we will use the following two components:

- Tokenizer Configuration files
- .NET Library

Let's start with downloading the tokenizer configuration files into the application directory by opening the following URL https:// huggingface.co/openai-community/gpt2/tree/main and downloading the following files from the website:

- vocab.json
- merges.txt

Note   These files are part of the GPT-2 tokenizer. The GPT-2 tokenizer is a byte-pair encoding (BPE) tokenizer. It works by splitting text into subword units (tokens) and using them as inputs for the GPT-2 model.

The vocab.json file contains a mapping of token IDs to token strings, for example, the words "the" and "of" will look like {"the": 0, "of": 1, ...}. The file defines the vocabulary of the tokenizer and made of 50,257 tokens.

The merges.txt contains a list of merge operations used to construct the tokens from individual characters.

If we take the following line, for example, "e s" means that the characters "e" and "s" can be merged into a single token "es".

The Tokenizer uses these merge operations recursively until no more merges are possible or the vocabulary limit is reached. The merges.txt file defines the rules of the tokenizer and determines how to split and join text into tokens.

Add Packages

After adding the Tokenizer files, we can add all the .NET packages we need for our project.

Open the project file aoi-ch3-app.csproj located in the application's main directory, and add the following code under the </PropertGroup> tag:

```
  <ItemGroup>
  <PackageReference Include="Azure.AI.OpenAI" Version="1.0.0-beta.6" />
  <PackageReference Include="Azure.Core" Version="1.38.0" />
  <PackageReference Include="Microsoft.Extensions.
  Configuration" Version="9.0.0-preview.2.24128.5" />
  <PackageReference Include="Microsoft.Extensions.
  Configuration.Json" Version="9.0.0-preview.2.24128.5" />
  <PackageReference Include="Microsoft.ML.Tokenizers"
  Version="0.21.1" />
  </ItemGroup>
```

After adding the software packages, the project file should look like this:

```
<Project Sdk="Microsoft.NET.Sdk">

  <PropertyGroup>
    <OutputType>Exe</OutputType>
    <TargetFramework>net8.0</TargetFramework>
    <RootNamespace>aoi_ch3_app</RootNamespace>
    <ImplicitUsings>enable</ImplicitUsings>
    <Nullable>enable</Nullable>
  </PropertyGroup>
```

```
  <ItemGroup>
  <PackageReference Include="Azure.AI.OpenAI"
  Version="1.0.0-beta.6" />
  <PackageReference Include="Azure.Core" Version="1.38.0" />
  <PackageReference Include="Microsoft.Extensions.
  Configuration" Version="9.0.0-preview.2.24128.5" />
  <PackageReference Include="Microsoft.Extensions.
  Configuration.Json" Version="9.0.0-preview.2.24128.5" />
  <PackageReference Include="Microsoft.ML.Tokenizers"
  Version="0.21.1" />
  </ItemGroup>

</Project>
```

You can also download the package using the following dotnet cli commands:

```
dotnet add package Azure.AI.OpenAI Version=1.0.0-beta.6
dotnet add package Azure.Core Version=1.38.0
dotnet add package  Microsoft.ML.Tokenizers Version="0.21.1
dotnet add package Microsoft.Extensions.Configuration
Version=9.0.0-preview.2.24128.5
dotnet add package  Microsoft.Extensions.Configuration.Json
Version=9.0.0-preview.2.24128.5
```

Add Code

In the final stage of creating our password generation application using Azure OpenAI and Azure SDK for .NET, we will add the actual C# code that will make up our application and the token counter code.

To start adding the code to our application, open the C# console application we created earlier and double-click the **Program.cs** file.

Copy the following code into the file (you will find the code in the repository of this book). The code also contains explanations about each section of the program.

```
/// This program demonstrates how to use Azure OpenAI to
generate secure passwords.

using System.Text;
using System.Text.Json;
using Microsoft.Extensions.Configuration;
using Microsoft.Extensions.Configuration.Json;
// Add the Azure namespace
using Azure;
// Add the OpenAI namespace
using Azure.AI.OpenAI;
using static System.Environment;
//  Add the Tokenizer namespace
using Microsoft.ML.Tokenizers;

// vocabulary files used to encode the text into tokens
var vocabFilePath = @"vocab.json";
var mergeFilePath = @"merges.txt";
var tokenizer = new Tokenizer(new Bpe(vocabFilePath,
mergeFilePath));

var AOAI_ENDPOINT = Environment.GetEnvironmentVariable("AOAI_
ENDPOINT");
var AOAI_KEY = Environment.GetEnvironmentVariable("AOAI_KEY");
var AOAI_DEPLOYMENTID = Environment.
GetEnvironmentVariable("AOAI_DEPLOYMENTID");

var endpoint = new Uri(AOAI_ENDPOINT);
var credentials = new Azure.AzureKeyCredential(AOAI_KEY);
var openAIClient = new OpenAIClient(endpoint, credentials);
```

```
// Define the system prompt for the AI
var systemPrompt = "You are a virtual AI that generates strong
and secure passwords";

// Define the user prompt for generating a secure password
var userPrompt =
    """

    Please generate a secure password with at least 20 characters.
    Please include at least one special character and
    one number.
    Please include a message regarding the password and its
    security.
    """;

//Completion options
var completionOptions = new ChatCompletionsOptions
{
    MaxTokens=100,
    Temperature=0.5f,
    FrequencyPenalty=0.0f,
    PresencePenalty=0.0f,
    NucleusSamplingFactor=1 // Top P
};

// Add system and user prompts to completion options
completionOptions.Messages.Add(new ChatMessage(ChatRole.System,
systemPrompt));
completionOptions.Messages.Add(new ChatMessage(ChatRole.User,
userPrompt));
// Get chat completions asynchronously
ChatCompletions response = await openAIClient.
GetChatCompletionsAsync(AOAI_DEPLOYMENTID, completionOptions);
// Print the generated password
```

```
Console.WriteLine(response.Choices.First().Message.Content);

// The user's input is taken and encoded using the tokenizer.
var input = userPrompt;
// The encoded result is stored in 'tokenizerEncodedResult'.
var tokenizerEncodedResult = tokenizer.Encode(input);
// The number of tokens used in the encoding is counted.
tokenizerEncodedResult.Tokens.Count();
// The console's foreground color is set to Magenta.
Console.ForegroundColor = ConsoleColor.Magenta;
// The number of tokens used is printed to the console in
Magenta color.
Console.WriteLine($"Number of tokens used:
{tokenizerEncodedResult.Tokens.Count()}");
// The console's color settings are reset to default.
Console.ResetColor();
```

The file structure of the application should be

```
Mode               LastWriteTime           Length Name
----               -------------           ------ ----
d----       15/05/2024 10:18 AM                   obj
-a---       15/05/2024 11:17 AM              769 aoi-ch3-
                                                 app.csproj
-a---       15/05/2024 11:00 AM           456318 merges.txt
-a---       16/05/2024  2:13 PM             2694 Program.cs
-a---       15/05/2024 11:00 AM          1042301 vocab.json
```

Save the Program.cs file and continue to the next section.

Create Environment Variables

Before we can run our application, we need to create environment variables that contain the information about the following:

- Azure OpenAI Resource endpoint

- API Key

- Deployment name

Environment variables are a set of key-value pairs that store the configuration and settings of an application. In our case, we will store the above three settings inside environment variables.

Environment variables can store information like

- API keys

- Endpoints

- Passwords

- Connection strings

They help us protect sensitive data, avoid hard-coding values, and enable easy switching between different environments, such as development, testing, or production.

To create environment variables on Windows, we will use PowerShell.

Note   In this book, I'm using temporary environment variables that are only available for the life of the session and deleted once the computer or VS code is restored.

With the information gathered from the View Code section, add your API key, Endpoint URL, and Deployment name to the code below and run each line in the VS Code terminal.

```
$env:AOAI_KEY ="API-KEY-VALUE"
$env:AOAI_ENDPOINT ="ENDPOINT URL"
$env:AOAI_DEPLOYMENTID ="DEPLOYMENT NAME"
```

In Figure 3-12, you can see my Terminal window in VS Code, where I run the PowerShell command that sets the environment variable for the AOAI_ENDPOINT.

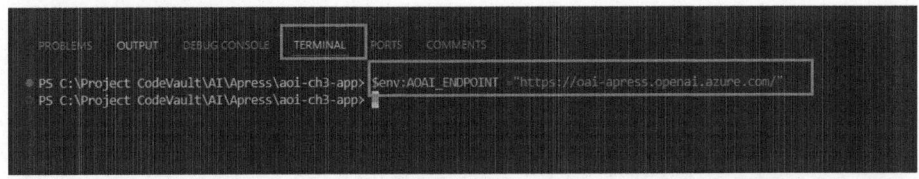

Figure 3-12. *Set environment variable using PowerShell and VS Code*

Please repeat this step for each environment variable.

After adding the environment variables, you can use the following command to verify that the environment variables were added successfully:

```
Get-ChildItem -Path Env:\AOAI_*
```

Run Application

It is time to run the application and see Azure OpenAI and GPT4 in action.

From the VS Code terminal window and from the path of our application, run the following command:

```
dotnet run
```

The output of the program should look like this:

```
Password: T3chS3cur!tyP@ssw0rd2022
```

Message: Your new password is strong and secure, containing a mix of uppercase and lowercase letters, numbers, and a special character. It is 25 characters long, which exceeds the minimum requirement of 20 characters. Remember to keep your password safe and avoid using it on multiple platforms to maintain its security.
Number of tokens used: 38

In Figure 3-13, I have a screenshot of the output.

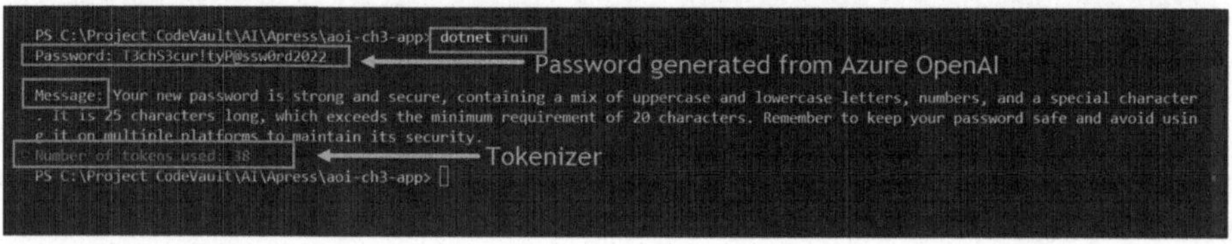

Figure 3-13. *Output*

In the output, the program uses the Azure OpenAI endpoint with the API key and asks for the GPT-4 model (with the deployment name of GPT-4) to generate a secure password with the following specifications stored in the Program.cs file (line 33 inside a variable called UserPrompt).

Please generate a secure password with at least 20 characters. Please include at least one special character and one number. Please include a message regarding the password and its security.

The GPT-4 model generates a secure password and returns it with an extra explanation about its complexity.

The last line of the code uses the Tokenizer library to count the tokens our request used and present it to the screen. In our case, the request used 38 tokens.

We can estimate the cost of the request by using the following formula (courtesy of ChatGPT), as shown in Figure 3-14, which is around $0.00114.

$$\text{Cost} = \frac{\text{Number of tokens}}{1000} \times \text{Price per 1,000 tokens}$$

For an 8K context window:

$$\text{Cost} = \frac{38}{1000} \times 0.03 = \$0.00114$$

For a 32K context window:

$$\text{Cost} = \frac{38}{1000} \times 0.06 = \$0.00228$$

Figure 3-14. *Calculation of token costs*

At this stage, our console application is working and also provides us with enough details about the number of tokens it uses for each request.

In the next section, we will cover how to deploy Azure OpenAI resources using Terraform, Azure CLI, and PowerShell.

The reason I'm adding these sections now is to give you a clear and consistent step-by-step and end-to-end guide on all the steps you need to get an application running with Azure OpenAI.

Using Terraform, Azure CLI, and PowerShell to create the services is optional.

Use Terraform to Create Azure OpenAI Resource and Deployment

In this section, we will look at how we can automate creating an Azure OpenAI resource and deployment using Terraform.

In Chapter 2, I explained how Terraform works and how to get started, so please refer to Chapter 2 if you need a refresher.

The following Terraform configuration code will do the following:

- Create a resource group on Azure.

- Create an Azure OpenAI resource (in the code, Azure OpenAI resource is called Cognitive account as per the previous brand of Azure AI).

- Azure OpenAI Deployment.

For your convenience, I have added comments to the code for each action. Review the comments after the # sign for more details.

Terraform Configuration (main.tf)

```
provider "azurerm" {
  features {}  # Provider block for Azure Resource Manager
}

resource "azurerm_resource_group" "example" {
  name     = "rg-apress-terraform-ai"  # Name of the
                                           resource group
  location = "east US"  # Location of the resource group
}

resource "azurerm_cognitive_account" "example" {
name  = "aoi-apress-terraform-ai"  # Name of the
                                      cognitive account
resource_group_name = azurerm_resource_group.example.name
# Name of the associated resource group
location  = azurerm_resource_group.example.location
# Location of the associated resource group
sku_name  = "SO"  # SKU name for the cognitive account
kind      = "OpenAI"  # Type of cognitive account
}
```

```
resource "azurerm_cognitive_deployment" "example" {
name                 = "gpt4"  # Name of the cognitive deployment
cognitive_account_id = azurerm_cognitive_account.example.id
# ID of the associated cognitive account

  model {
    format  = "OpenAI"  # Format of the model
    name    = "gpt-4"  # Name of the model
    #version = "0613"  # Version of the model (commented out)
  }

  scale {
    type = "Standard"  # Type of scaling for the deployment
  }
}
```

To deploy the Terraform configuration in VS Code, use the following steps.

Deploy Using Terraform

Create a directory called OpenAI:

```
mkdir openai
```

Open a terminal window in VS Code, and open the location from the terminal window.

Before deploying resources to Azure using Terraform, we must authenticate to Azure using Azure CLI. Before deploying the code, make sure you authenticate to Azure with a user that has enough permissions to create resources on the subscription.

To authenticate, use the following Azure CLI command:

```
az login
```

Note   If you are using WSL or a Linux host without a GUI, use `az login -use-device-code`.

Once you pass the authentication stage, we can initialize Terraform using

```
terraform init
```

Next, run the plan command and review the changes

```
terraform plan
```

To deploy the Azure OpenAI resource and deployment run

```
terraform apply
```

Verify Deployment

If you open the Microsoft Aure portal, go to the Azure AI Services section, and click view under Azure OpenAI, you will see the newly created resource as shown in Figure 3-15.

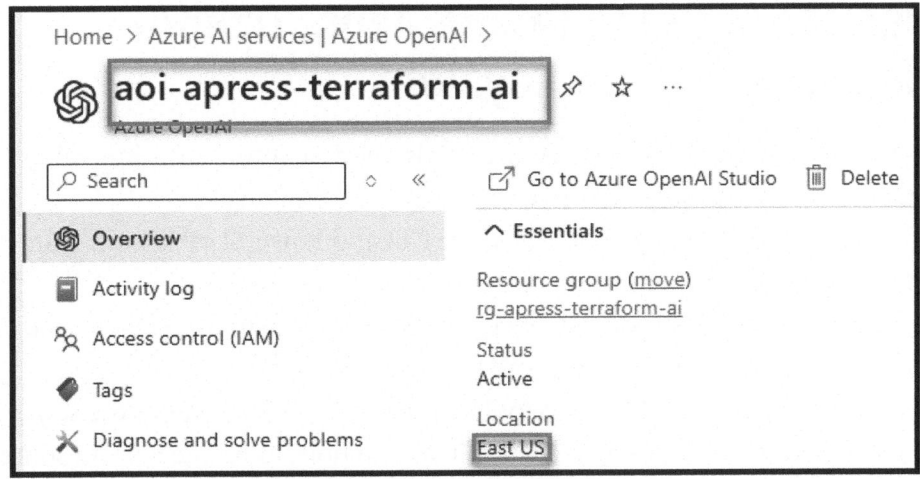

Figure 3-15. *Azure OpenAI resource*

If you click the Go to Azure OpenAI Studio on the top menu, follow the link to the portal, and click deployment, you will see the newly created OpenAI model deployment, as shown in Figure 3-16.

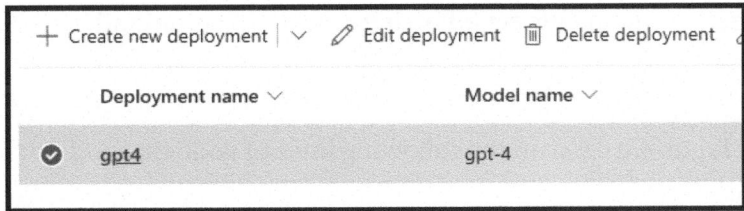

Figure 3-16. *Deployment*

Destroy Deployment

To delete the deployed resources using Terraform, run the following command:

```
terraform destroy
```

Use Azure CLI to Create Azure OpenAI Resource and Deployment

As we discussed in Chapter 2, Azure CLI is another command-line utility that helps us to manage Azure resources programmatically.

The main difference between Azure CLI and PowerShell is that Azure CLI is written in Python, while PowerShell is written in .NET.

People with Windows and .NET experience prefer to use PowerShell, while people with Paython will find it easier to use Azure CLI.

The functionality of the two tools is the same, and both offer the same feature set. I recommend you get familiar with both tools because, in some cases, creating a resource with Azure CLI or PowerShell can be simpler and require fewer lines of code than others.

Create Resources

To create an Azure OpenAI Resource and deploy a model, let's start by logging in to Azure using the following Azure CLI command:

```
az login
```

After login, we can run the following lines of code that will do the following:

- Create an Azure Resource Group in the EastUS region.

- Create an Azure OpenAI resource named aoi-apress-ai.

- Create an Azure OpenAI deployment using GPT-4 model.

```
# Create an Azure resource group

az group create --name rg-apress-ai --location eastus
```

```
# Create an Azure OpenAI resource

az cognitiveservices account create  --name aoi-apress-ai
--location eastus --resource-group rg-apress-ai --kind OpenAI
--sku S0

# Create an Azure OpenAI deployment
az cognitiveservices account deployment create --name aoi-
apress-ai --resource-group rg-apress-ai --deployment-name
gpt-4 --model-name gpt-4 --model-format OpenAI --model-version
0613   --sku-name "Standard" --sku-capacity "1"
```

Before you run the code, I recommend you install the Azure CLI Tools extension shown in Figure 3-17.

Figure 3-17. *Azure CLI Tools VS Code extension*

Azure CLI Tools

With the Azure CLI Tools extension, we can create .azcli files that contain the Azure CLI command.

Once creating a .azcli file, the extension offers the following:

- IntelliSense for Azure CLI commands

- Built-in Snippets for Azure CLI commands

- Right-click and run Azure CLI commands in the terminal

- Review Azure CLI documentation about a command

Run Azure CLI Code

To deploy the above code, copy it to VS Code, and save the file with the .azcli extension.

Highlight the Azure CLI code, right-click on the code, and select Run Line in Terminal as shown in Figure 3-18.

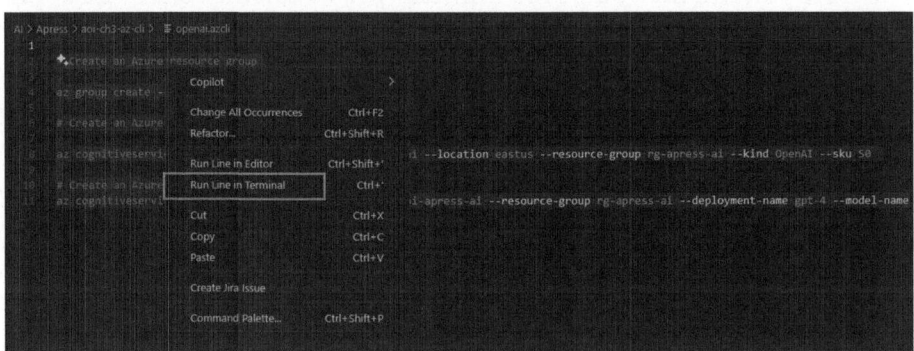

Figure 3-18. *Run Line in Terminal*

This will run the code and deploy the services.

Learn More About Azure CLI AI Services

To read more about the Azure CLI, `az cognitiveservices` command, and capabilities, visit the following URL:

https://learn.microsoft.com/en-us/cli/azure/cognitiveservices?view=azure-cli-latest

As you can see in Figure 3-18a, the command allows us to manage any aspect of an Azure OpenAI deployment and model.

Commands

Expand table

Name	Description	Type	Status
az cognitiveservices account	Manage Azure Cognitive Services accounts.	Core	GA
az cognitiveservices account commitment-plan	Manage commitment plans for Azure Cognitive Services accounts.	Core	GA
az cognitiveservices account commitment-plan create	Create a commitment plan for Azure Cognitive Services account.	Core	GA
az cognitiveservices account commitment-plan delete	Delete a commitment plan from Azure Cognitive Services account.	Core	GA
az cognitiveservices account commitment-plan list	Show all commitment plans from Azure Cognitive Services account.	Core	GA
az cognitiveservices account commitment-plan show	Show a commitment plan from Azure Cognitive Services account.	Core	GA
az cognitiveservices account create	Manage Azure Cognitive Services accounts.	Core	GA
az cognitiveservices account delete	Manage Azure Cognitive Services accounts.	Core	GA
az cognitiveservices account deployment	Manage deployments for Azure Cognitive Services accounts.	Core	GA
az cognitiveservices account deployment create	Create a deployment for Azure Cognitive Services account.	Core	GA
az cognitiveservices account deployment delete	Delete a deployment from Azure Cognitive Services account.	Core	GA
az cognitiveservices account deployment list	Show all deployments for Azure Cognitive Services account.	Core	GA
az cognitiveservices account deployment show	Show a deployment for Azure Cognitive Services account.	Core	GA
az cognitiveservices account identity	Manage identity of Cognitive Services accounts.	Core	GA
az cognitiveservices account identity assign	Assign an identity of a Cognitive Services account.	Core	GA
az cognitiveservices account identity remove	Remove the identity from a Cognitive Services account.	Core	GA
az cognitiveservices account identity show	Show the identity of a Cognitive Services account.	Core	GA
az cognitiveservices account keys	Manage Azure Cognitive Services accounts.	Core	GA
az cognitiveservices account keys list	Manage Azure Cognitive Services accounts.	Core	GA
az cognitiveservices account keys regenerate	Manage Azure Cognitive Services accounts.	Core	GA
az cognitiveservices account list	Manage Azure Cognitive Services accounts.	Core	GA
az cognitiveservices account list-deleted	List soft-deleted Azure Cognitive Services accounts.	Core	GA

Figure 3-18a. *Azure az cognitiveservices command*

Use Azure PowerShell to Create Azure OpenAI Resource and Deployment

The last deployment method I will cover is using Azure PowerShell. Azure PowerShell allows us to deploy resources to Azure using cmdlets, and it is mainly used in automation runbooks.

In Chapter 2, we covered the process of installing the Azure PowerShell module, so please refer to the chapter for more details.

Before commencing the deployment, I recommend you update the module to the latest version using the following cmdlet.

Create Resources

Open a terminal window in VS Code.

Type the following command to start using PowerShell 7:

```
pwsh
```

To update the Azure PowerShell module, run

```
Update-Module -Name Az -Force
```

To connect to Azure, type

```
Connect-AzAccount
```

If you're using WSL, use

```
Connect-AzAccount -UseDeviceAuthentication
```

If you have more than one Azure subscription, you can't set it using

```
Set-AzContext -SubscriptionId "SubscriptionId"
```

We are ready to deploy an Azure OpenAI resource and model.

For this exercise, I prepared a PowerShell script with comments explaining each step of the deployment process.

PowerShell Script: Aoi-deploy.ps1

The script follows the following process:

- Declare variables.

- Connect to Azure.

- Create a new resource group.

- Create an Azure OpenAI resource.

- Create Azure OpenAI deployment for a GPT-4 model.

```
$rgname ="rg-apress-ai" # Resource group name
$location = "eastus" # Location
$aoiresource = "ai-apress-az-powershell" # Cognitive Services
                                         account name

Connect-AzAccount # Connect to Azure account

New-AzResourceGroup -Name $rgname -Location $location
# Create a new resource group

# Create a new Cognitive Services account
New-AzCognitiveServicesAccount -ResourceGroupName $rgname -Name
$aoiresource -Type OpenAI -SkuName S0 -Location $location

$model = New-Object -TypeName 'Microsoft.Azure.Management.
CognitiveServices.Models.DeploymentModel' -Property @{
    Name = 'gpt-4' # Model name
    Version = '0613' # Model version
```

```
    Format = 'OpenAI' # Model format

}


$properties = New-Object -TypeName 'Microsoft.Azure.Management.
CognitiveServices.Models.DeploymentProperties' -Property @{
    Model = $model
}

$sku = New-Object -TypeName "Microsoft.Azure.Management.
CognitiveServices.Models.Sku" -Property @{
    Name = 'Standard' # SKU name
    Capacity = '1' # SKU capacity

}


# Deploy the model to the Cognitive Services account
New-AzCognitiveServicesAccountDeployment -ResourceGroupName
$rgname -AccountName $aoiresource -Name "gpt-4" -Properties
$properties -sku $sku
```

Retrieve Information

If you would like to retrieve the following details about the deployment

- Endpoint URL

- Access Key

- Resource details

Run the following cmdlets:

```
# Reterive the endpoint and key of the Cognitive
Services account
```

```
Get-AzCognitiveServicesAccount -ResourceGroupName $rgname -Name
$aoiresource | Select-Object -Property endpoint
Get-AzCognitiveServicesAccountKey -Name $aoiresource
-ResourceGroupName $rgname |  Select-Object -Property Key1
Get-AzCognitiveServicesAccount -ResourceGroupName $rgname -Name
$aoiresource | ft
```

Delete Deployment

To delete the deployment, please use the following PowerShell script:

```
$rgname ="rg-apress-powershell1" # Resource group name
$location = "eastus" # Location
$aoiresource = "aiapresspowershell1" # Cognitive Services
                                     account name
# Remove the deployment of the GPT-4 model from the Cognitive
Services account
Remove-AzCognitiveServicesAccountDeployment -ResourceGroupName
$rgname -AccountName $aoiresource -Name GPT-4

# Remove the Cognitive Services account itself
Remove-AzCognitiveServicesAccount -Name $aoiresource
-ResourceGroupName $rgname
```

Use Azure OpenAI with Postman

Postman is the world's most popular API Platform and the developer of the Postman API Desktop and web client.

Postman has over 30 million registered users and 500,000 organizations that use it.

Besides offering a development platform for APIs, it also offers a simple interface to connect to REST API (Representational State Transfer Application Programming Interface) endpoints.

RESTful APIs use HTTP requests to perform the following CRUD operations:

- Create

- Read

- Update

- Delete

The above operations correspond to

- GET

- PUT

- POST

- PATCH

- DELETE

In the following table, you can see how CRUD operations correspond to REST API operations.

Operation (CRUD)	Operation (REST)	Description
CREATE	POST	Create a new resource
UPDATE	PUT	Update existing resource
UPDATE	PATCH	Partially update a resource
READ	GET	Retrieve data from
DELETE	DELETE	Delete

In the case of Azure OpenAI, we can use Postman (or another REST API client like curl) to send requests to an Azure OpenAI endpoint and test prompts and responses.

The main use case for using Postman and REST APIs with Azure OpenAI is that it offers a simple testing platform to test the functionality and usability of an endpoint.

With Postman, we can test and develop API requests using Postman's intuitive interface and quickly build prototype APIs before starting the development process of applications.

We can also automate testing of APIs using Postman's built-in testing platform. And most importantly collaborate with team members during the development cycle of an API.

In Chapter 2, we installed Postman, so please refer to the Postman's installation steps if you need to.

Configure Workspace

Let's start with opening the Postman Desktop client or the web client (in this lab, I will be using the Postman web client).

Go to Postman.com.

Click Workspaces.

Click Create a new Workspace to create a new one, or click My Workspace to use the default workspace, as shown in Figure 3-19.

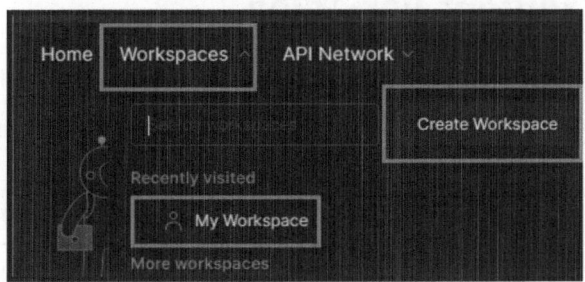

Figure 3-19. *Open a Postman's workspace*

Create an Environment

From the left side menu, click Environments, as shown in Figure 3-20.

Figure 3-20. *Environments*

In Postman, we use environments to store environment variables like API keys, endpoint URLs, and more.

Click on the + sign to create a new environment with the following details.

Name	Azure OpenAI

Add Environment Variables

Your environment should have the following variables. Add the Azure OpenAI API key and Endpoint URL details to the environment.

Variable	Type	Initial Value	Current Value
AZURE_OPENAI_KEY	Default	API Key	API Key
AZURE_OPENAI_ENDPOINT	Default	Endpoint URL	Endpoint URL

Figure 3-21 shows the environment variables screen in Postman. After adding the variables, make sure you click Save.

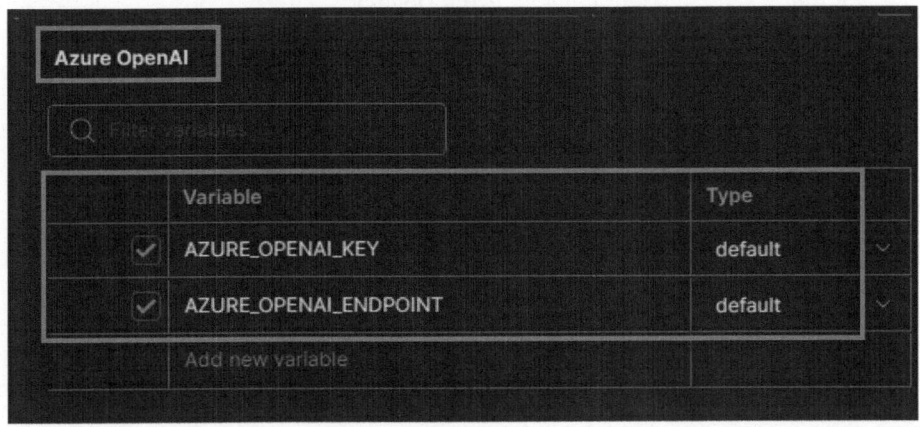

Figure 3-21. *Environment variables*

The next step is to create an API request.

Create a Collection

Click the Collections tab, as shown in Figure 3-22.

Figure 3-22. *Collections tab*

Click the + sign and create a new collection with the following name.

Name	Azure OpenAI

Create a POST Request

After creating the collection, let's create our first API call to Azure OpenAI by right-clicking the collection name and selecting Add request.

Every API request in Postman has the following tables (Figure 3-23).

- Params

- Authorization

- Headers

- Body

- Scripts

- Settings

Figure 3-23. *Request options*

In this lab, we will focus on the Authorization and Body options.

The first thing we need to do is add our API key to the request. We do that by setting the Auth type to API Key and referencing the environment variable we created earlier.

Click the Authorization tab and use the following settings as shown in Figure 3-24.

Auth Type	API Key
Key	Api-key
Value	{{Azure_OPENAI_KEY}}
Add to	Header

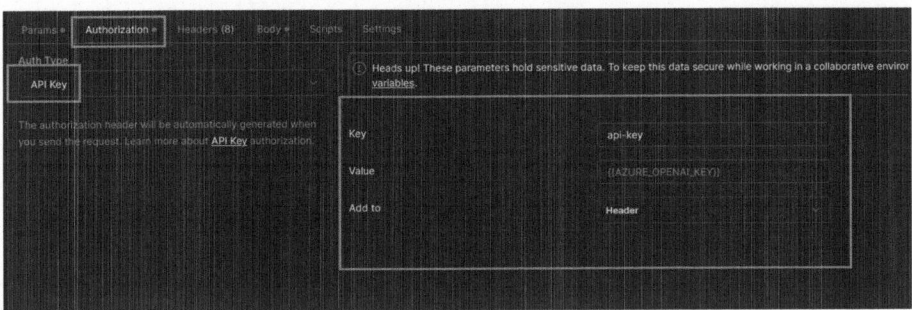

Figure 3-24. *Authorization screen*

Run POST Request

Now that we have the authorization section sorted, let's focus on the request body, which will store the prompt we send to the GPT-4 model.

Click on the Body tab, and add the following JSON formatted body.

```
{
"messages":[{"role": "system", "content": "You are an AI
assistant."},
{"role": "assistant", "content": "How do I use environment
variables with Azure CLI"}]
}
```

The JSON request has a chat completion request body that uses the OpenAI request body. You can visit the OpenAI API reference page using the following URL https://platform.openai.com/docs/api-reference/chat/create.

In a nutshell, the request body is made of a list of messages (system, user, assistance, and tool). In our example, we are using a system and a user message.

Figure 3-25 shows the Body request in Postman.

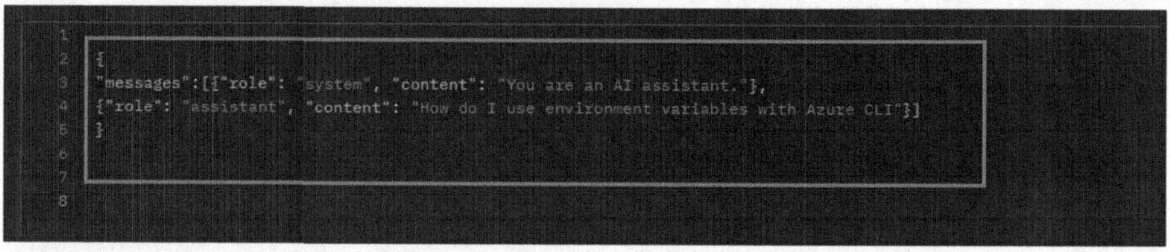

Figure 3-25. *Body request*

Now, it's finally time to work on the POST request and send our prompt to an Azure OpenAI endpoint.

In the request Window, add the following API call.

Request	`{{AZURE_OPENAI_ENDPOINT}}/openai/deployments/DEPLOYMENTNAME/chat/completions?api-version=2024-02-15-preview&Content-Type=application/json`

The request URL is made of the following:

Azure OpenAI Endpoint	`{{AZURE_OPENAI_ENDPOINT}}`
URL Path 1	`/openai/deployments`
Azure OpenAI Deployment Name	`DEPLOYMENTNAME`
URL Path 2	`/chat/completions?`
API Version	`?api-version=2024-02-15-preview`
Request Content type	`&Content-Type=application/json`

The main takeaway is to make sure you are setting the following values:

- Azure OpenAI Endpoint

- Azure OpenAI Deployment Name

- API Version

Figure 3-26 shows the request URL.

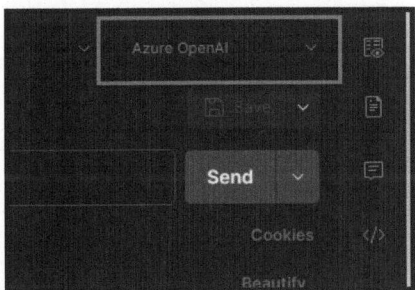

Figure 3-26. *Request URL*

Before running the request, make sure you set the collection to use the Azure OpenAI environment by using the drop-down menu in the top right corner, as shown in Figure 3-26a.

Figure 3-26a. *Set environment*

To run the request, click Send and review the response body (set to Pretty), as shown in Figure 3-27.

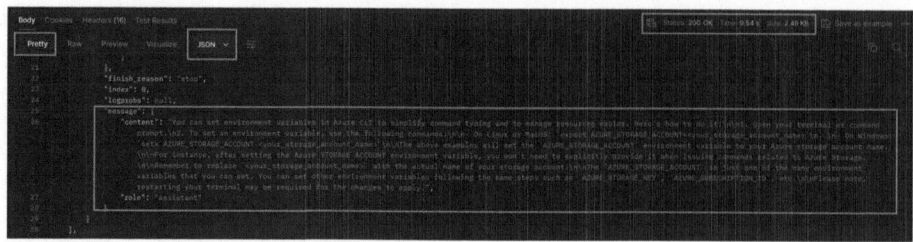

Figure 3-27. *Response body from Azure OpenAI*

The response body will provide us with the reply in the message section of the body, the status of the reply, and the amount of time it took Azure OpenAI to provide it.

List Models

If you want to list all the available OpenAI models in Azure OpenAI, you can run the following API request:

```
{{AZURE_OPENAI_ENDPOINT}}/openai/models?api-
version=2024-02-15-preview
```

You can review the request URL in Figure 3-28.

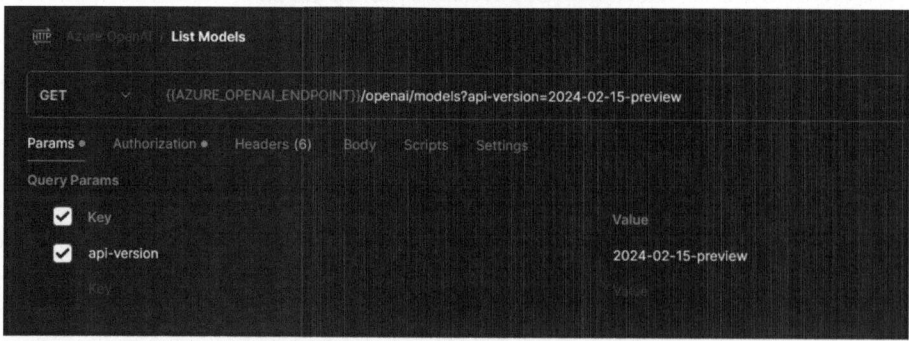

Figure 3-28. *List OpenAI models in Azure OpenAI*

Please don't forget to add your API key to the Authorization tab. Also, note that Postman automatically creates Query Params, which we can change from the Params tab (shown in Figure 3-28).

API Resources

Remember to check and also set the right API version of the OpenAI service by using the following URL `https://learn.microsoft.com/en-us/rest/api/azureopenai/operation-groups?view=rest-azureopenai-2024-02-15-preview` and using the drop-down menu of the top left corner as shown in Figure 3-29.

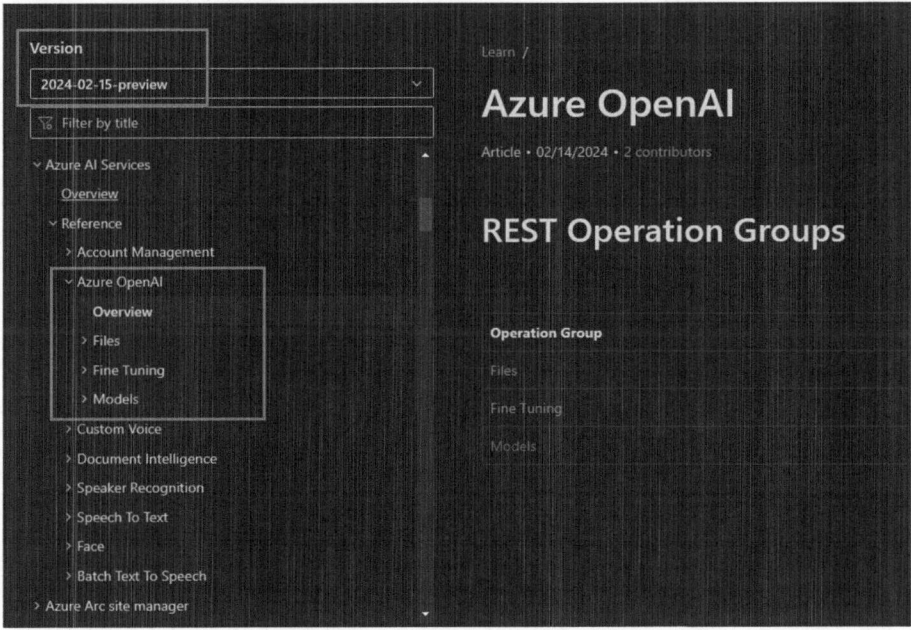

Figure 3-29. *Azure OpenAI API Versions*

Chapter Summary

This chapter focused on deploying an Azure OpenAI resource and GPT-4 Model using the following tools:

- Azure Portal

- Azure PowerShell

- Azure CLI

- Terraform

We also created a C# console application that uses a GPT-4 model to generate a secure password and count tokens.

The concept of the console application is just an example of how we can use Azure OpenAI using .NET.

The main takeaway of this chapter is to understand the end-to-end process of deploying all the necessary infrastructure and resources for an application that utilizes Azure OpenAI.

We also learned how to use Postman with an Azure OpenAI endpoint and send prompts to a GPT-4 model.

Before moving on to the next chapter, ensure you understand the process and tools we used.

It is important you understand the use case of each tool; for example, if your use case is to provision many Azure OpenAI environments that are similar to each other, use Terraform.

CHAPTER 4

.NET SDK and AI Studio

This chapter will turn our C# console app into a web application running on ASP.NET.

The application will use the Azure OpenAI deployment and model we used in Chapter 3.

For this exercise, we will use some of the tools we covered in Chapter 2, so please make sure you have all the tools installed and configured on your machine.

Create ASP.NET Application with Azure OpenAI

In this section, we will create an ASP.NET application that uses an Azure OpenAI resource and GPT-4 model to generate secure passwords.

The app uses the same backend as the C# console in Chapter 3, with added functionality and a web interface.

In Figure 4-1, you can see the result of the application. You will find the source code in the book's repository.

© The Editor(s) (if applicable) and The Author(s),
under exclusive license to APress Media, LLC, part of Springer Nature 2024
S. Ifrah, *Getting Started with Azure OpenAI*, https://doi.org/10.1007/979-8-8688-0599-8_4

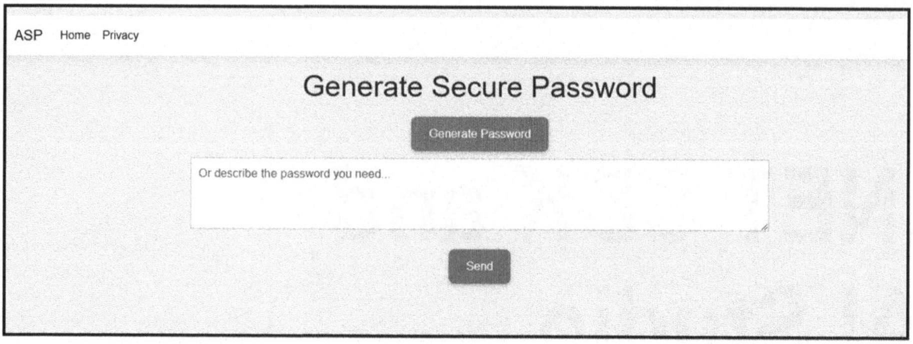

Figure 4-1. *ASP.NET application*

To create the application, follow the steps below.

Create an ASP.NET Application

To get started, we first need to create an ASP.NET application.

From the VS Code terminal windows, run the following command:

```
dotnet new webapp -n ASP-APP
```

The structure of the app should look like Figure 4-2.

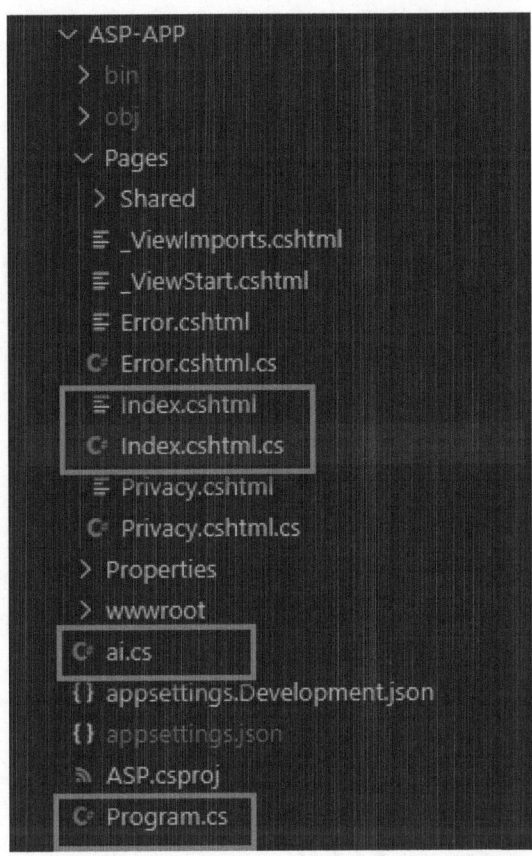

Figure 4-2. *Application structure*

The main components of the app are as follows.

Program.cs	This is the entry point file to the application
ai.cs	C# Class where Azure OpenAI settings and prompts are configured
Index.cshtml	HTML and Razor configuration
	This Razor and HTML file acts as the user interface and home page of the application
	The file contains a page model and defines an OnGet method for anti-forgery tokens
	It includes custom CSS styles for the page layout
	The file contains a form and a JavaScript function to copy the generated password and chat response to the clipboard
Index.cshtml.cs	Code-behind Razor page. Hold the definitions of two properties (SecurePassword and ChatResponse) that store the generated password.
	The file also contains the definitions of two methods that handle POST requests for generating the passwords

Install Azure OpenAI Library

This application also uses the Azure OpenAI class library. To install it. from the VS Code terminal, run the following command:

```
dotnet add package Azure.AI.OpenAI --version 1.0.0-beta.8
```

Create Class

To create a C# Class, right click on application's folder in vs Code and create a new file with the following details.

Name	ai.cs

Inside the file, we define a class called AI that interacts with the Azure OpenAI service to generate secure passwords.

The class contains a single method called CallAI that uses the following environment variables:

- AOAI_ENDPOINT

- AOAI_KEY

- AOAI_DEPLOYMENTID

These variables contain the details of our Azure OpenAI resource and OpenAI deployment name. We used the variables in Chapter 3 to build the C# console application.

We then create an instance of the OpenAIClient class using the variables above and authenticate to the Azure OpenAI service.

The rest of the file configures the prompt and sends the request to GPT-4 model.

Class Configuration

The following code shows the class configuration in the ai.cs file:

- The code does the following:

- Use the Azure OpenAI library.

- Get the environment variables.

- Create an instance of the AIClient.

- Set the Completions options AI model.

- Set the System prompt and set it to the model.

- Returns the output from the model.

You can review the code and comments of each code block.

```
using Azure.AI.OpenAI;
using System.Threading.Tasks;

// Represents an AI class that interacts with an AI model to
generate secure passwords.

public class ai
{

// Calls the AI model to generate a secure password based on
the user input.
// The user input to generate the password
// Returns the generated secure password
    public async Task<string> CallAI(string userInput)
    {
        // Get the required environment variables
        var AOAI_ENDPOINT = Environment.GetEnvironment
        Variable("AOAI_ENDPOINT");
        var AOAI_KEY = Environment.GetEnvironment
        Variable("AOAI_KEY");
        var AOAI_DEPLOYMENTID = Environment.GetEnvironment
        Variable("AOAI_DEPLOYMENTID");

        // Create the AI client
        var endpoint = new Uri(AOAI_ENDPOINT);
        var credentials = new Azure.AzureKeyCredential
        (AOAI_KEY);
        var openAIClient = new OpenAIClient(endpoint, credentials);

        // Set the completion options for the AI model
        var completionOptions = new ChatCompletionsOptions
        {
```

```
        MaxTokens = 300,
        Temperature = 0.5f,
        FrequencyPenalty = 0.0f,
        PresencePenalty = 0.0f,
        NucleusSamplingFactor = 1 // Top P
    };

    // Set the system prompt and user input for the
    AI model
    var systemPrompt = "You're an AI Secure Password
    Generator. Please generate a secure password for me.
    password size can't be more than 40 characters. Only
    output the password without any other text.";
    completionOptions.Messages.Add(new ChatMessage
    (ChatRole.System, systemPrompt));
    completionOptions.Messages.Add(new ChatMessage
    (ChatRole.User, userInput));

    // Get the chat completions from the AI model
    ChatCompletions response = await openAIClient.
    GetChatCompletionsAsync(AOAI_DEPLOYMENTID,
    completionOptions);

    // Return the generated password
    return response.Choices.First().Message.Content;
    }
}
```

The remaining two important files are

- Index.cshtml

- Index.cshtml.cs

For reference, I have the Index.cshtml.cs file with comments. This file handles the part of the MVC (Model-View-Controller) pattern and is responsible for managing the logic behind the Index.cshtml Razor page.

```
using Microsoft.AspNetCore.Mvc;
using Microsoft.AspNetCore.Mvc.RazorPages;
using System.Threading.Tasks;

namespace ASP.Pages
{
   public class IndexModel : PageModel
{
    public string SecurePassword { get; set; }
    public string ChatResponse { get; set; }  // Added to hold
                                                  the response from
                                                  the chat

    public void OnGet()
    {
    }

    public async Task<IActionResult> OnPostAsync()
    {
        ai aiClient = new ai();
        SecurePassword = await aiClient.CallAI("create a 20
        chars password only and only output the password
        without any other text.");
        return Page();
    }

    // New handler for processing chat input
    public async Task<IActionResult> OnPostGeneratePasswordAsync
    (string userInput)
{
```

```
// Check if userInput is null or empty and provide a
default value or handle the case appropriately
if (string.IsNullOrEmpty(userInput))
{
    ChatResponse = "Please enter a valid input.";
    return Page();
}

ai aiClient = new ai();
try
{
    ChatResponse = await aiClient.CallAI(userInput);
}
catch (Exception ex)
{
    // Handle the exception, maybe log it, and provide a
    user-friendly message
    ChatResponse = "Failed to generate a password due to an
    internal error.";
    // Log the exception details here, ex.ToString()
}
return Page();
}

}

}
```

Run Web Application

To run the application, make sure you have set the environment variables by running the following commands:

```
$env:AOAI_KEY ="API-KEY-VALUE"
$env:AOAI_ENDPOINT ="ENDPOINT URL"
$env:AOAI_DEPLOYMENTID ="DEPLOYMENT NAME"
```

To check if the environment variables are set correctly, run this command:

```
Get-ChildItem -Path Env:\AOAI_*
```

To run the application, run

```
dotnet run
```

The terminal should display the path to the application (http://localhost:5113).

```
info: Microsoft.Hosting.Lifetime[14]
      Now listening on: http://localhost:5113
info: Microsoft.Hosting.Lifetime[0]
      Application started. Press Ctrl+C to shut down.
info: Microsoft.Hosting.Lifetime[0]
      Hosting environment: Development
info: Microsoft.Hosting.Lifetime[0]
      Content root path: C:\Project CodeVault\ASP-APP
```

Click the link while holding the Ctrl key on your keyboard, and your browser should open the application, as shown in Figure 4-3.

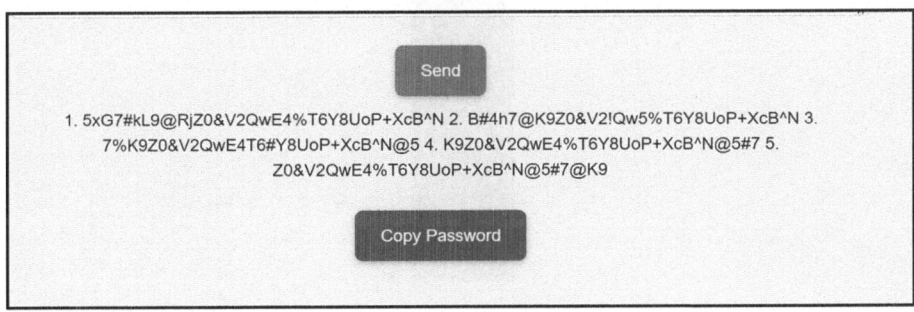

Figure 4-3. *Generate Secure Password*

You can use the text box to ask the model to generate a number of passwords or a very specific password.

In Figure 4-4, I asked the model to generate five passwords.

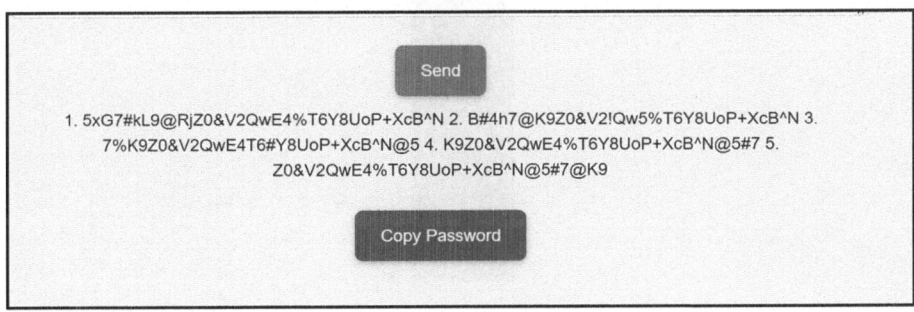

Figure 4-4. *Ask the model to generate passwords*

Create a Web App Using VS Code

Until now, all our applications run on our local computer, and since this book is about Microsoft Azure, we can easily extend our capabilities to deploy our ASP.NET applications to an Azure Web App.

Since we already have all the necessary tools (see Chapter 2) to deploy services to Azure, we can now take advantage of them and run our applications in Azure.

We will start by creating a web app in Azure using VS Code and then deploying the app.

From VS Code, Click on the Azure Tools icon on the left menu as shown in Figure 4-5.

Figure 4-5. *Azure Tools icon*

From the Azure Tools menu, click the App Services icon, as shown in Figure 4-6.

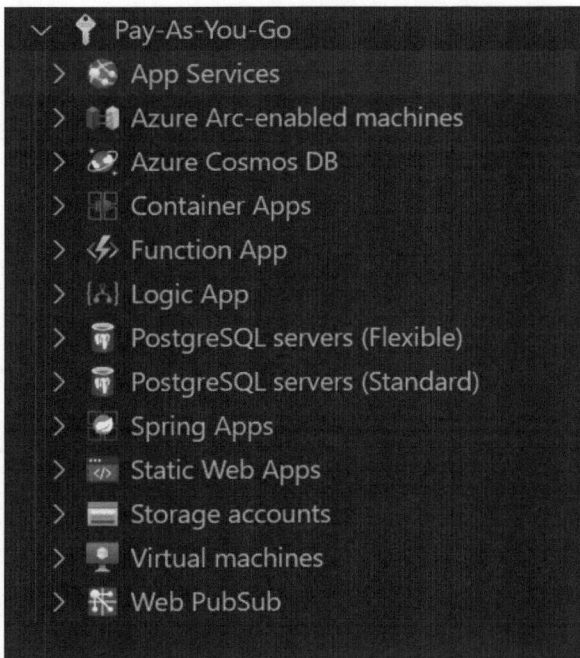

Figure 4-6. *Azure App Services*

Select the first option, Create Web App, as shown in Figure 4-7.

Figure 4-7. *Create Web App*

In the Create New Web App menu, name the Web App as follows and as shown in Figure 4-8.

Name	app-apress-asp

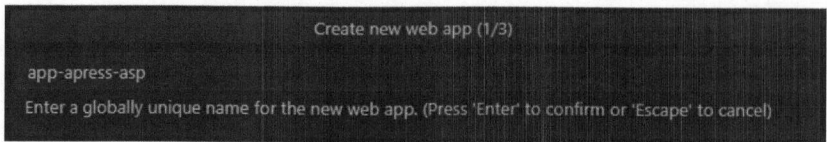

Figure 4-8. *Create a new Web App*

In the Select a runtime stack window, select .NET 8 (LTS), as shown in Figure 4-8a.

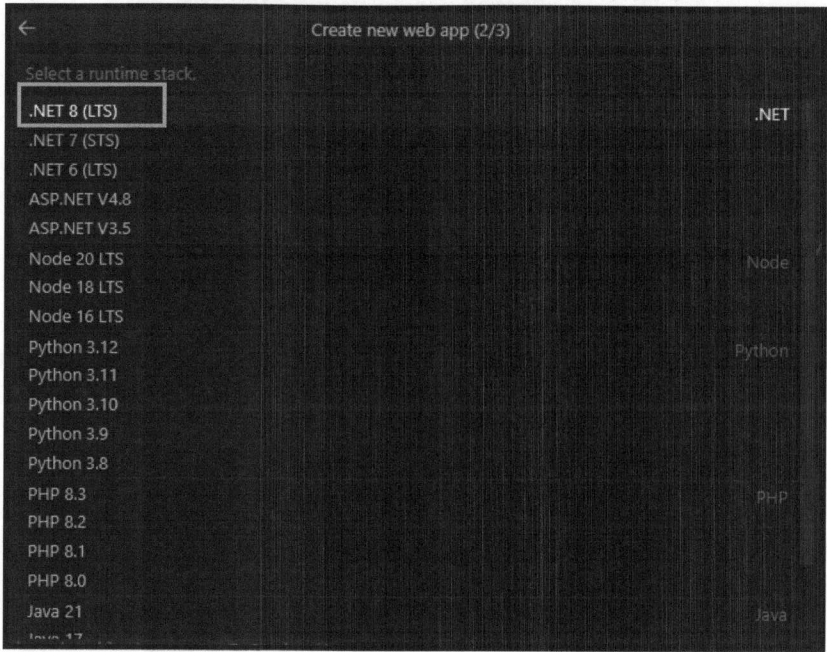

Figure 4-8a. *Runtime stack window*

In the Pricing tier selection window (Figure 4-9), select Premium (P1v2).

144

Figure 4-9. Pricing tier window

After selecting the pricing tier, Azure will start deploying the Web App Service. You can monitor the status of the deployment from the Activity Log terminal window, as shown in Figure 4-10.

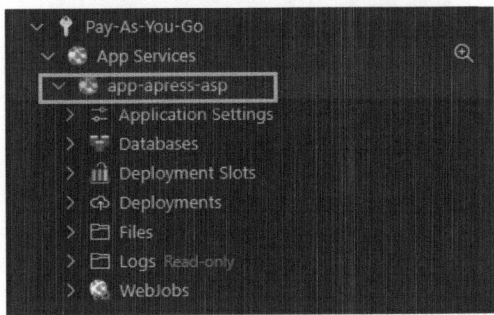

Figure 4-10. Activity Log

To view the newly created Web App, expand the App Services node, under the Azure Tools window, and you will see it as shown in Figure 4-11.

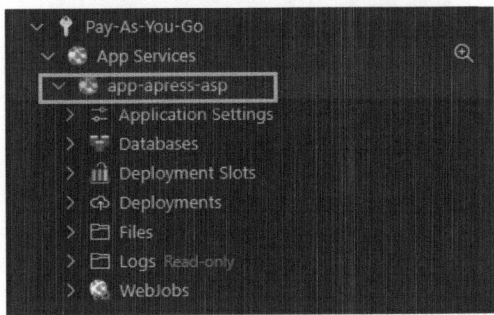

Figure 4-11. App Services node after deployment

Publish Application

Before deploying our application to Azure, we need to publish the app using the dotnet publish command.

The command will create a deployment folder with all the files a web server needs to run a .NET application.

To run an ASP.NET application, we need to create a release using the dotnet publish command. At the end of the process, we will have a .DLL file that contains all the libraries the Azure Web App will need to run the app.

To publish the app, open a VS Code terminal session in the location of the app's directory and run.

```
dotnet publish -c Release -o ./bin/Publish
```

You can see the result under the /Bin/Publish folder in the app's directory (shown in Figure 4-11a).

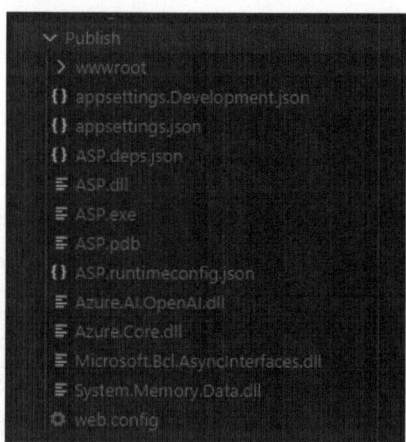

Figure 4-11a. *Publish folder*

Deploy to Web App

Now, we are ready to deploy our application to Azure Web App. At this stage, we have the following:

- App Service Plan

- Web App

- Published application (using dotnet published)

Note   Each Azure Web App needs an App Service Plan. An App Service Plan is an Azure hosting service that hosts Web App. In our case, Azure created one for us when we created a Web App.

To deploy our app to Azure Web App, right-click the Publish folder and select Deploy to Web App, as shown in Figure 4-12.

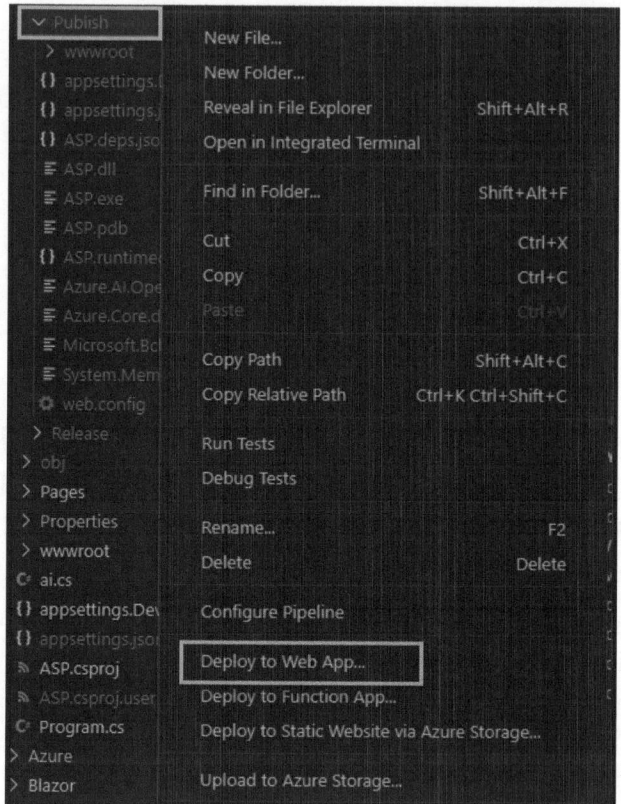

Figure 4-12. *Deploy to Web App*

VS Code will ask you to select the Azure subscription, as shown in Figure 4-13.

Figure 4-13. *Select subscription*

In the select resource screen, select the web app we created before as shown in Figure 4-14.

Figure 4-14. *Select resource*

In the overwrite prompt in Figure 4-15, select Deploy.

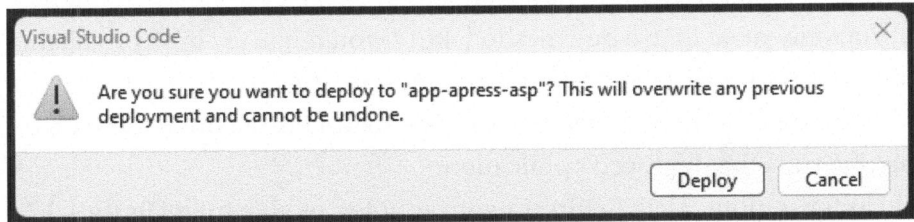

Figure 4-15. *Overwrite previous deployment*

You can monitor the deployment from the Activity Log window, as shown in Figure 4-16.

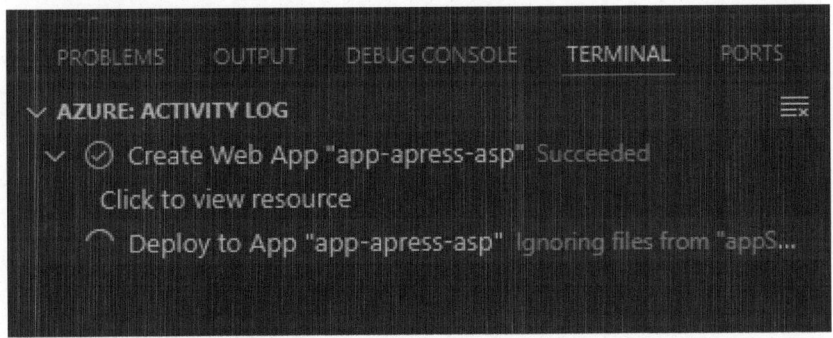

Figure 4-16. *Activity log*

149

Set Environment Variables Azure Web App

Once the application is deployed to Azure, it is running but not working yet. We must set the environment variables to get the application to work and connect to the Azure OpenAI endpoint.

In the last section of the deployment, we will set the environment variables. I will show you how to set the environment variables using the Azure portal, Azure CLI and PowerShell.

You only need to use one method, but I would like to show you all the available options as each will fit a different scenario.

To set environment variables using the Azure Portal, open the Web App that runs the deployed application.

Under settings, click Environment variables, as shown in Figure 4-17.

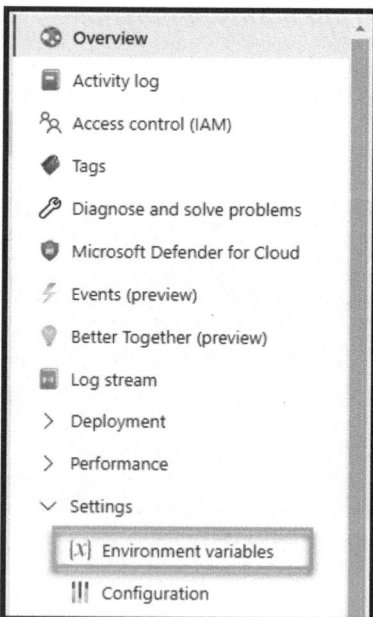

Figure 4-17. *Environment variables*

We will add the following environment variables:

```
$env:AOAI_KEY ="API-KEY-VALUE"
$env:AOAI_ENDPOINT ="ENDPOINT URL"
$env:AOAI_DEPLOYMENTID ="DEPLOYMENT NAME"
```

Click Add and add a new environment variable from the environment variables page, also known as application settings, as shown in Figure 4-18.

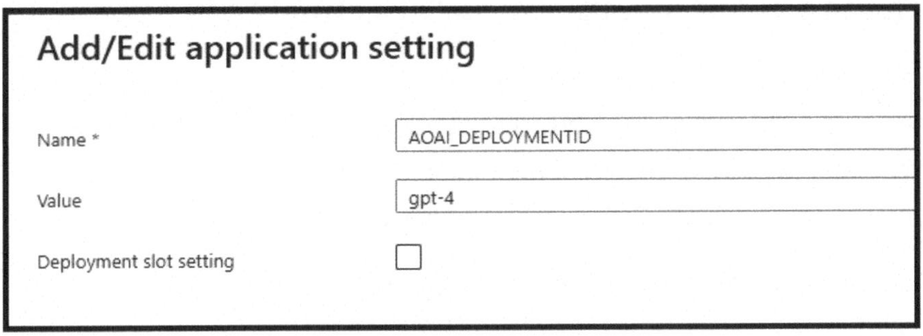

Figure 4-18. *Add/Edit application setting*

The values should be set as this.

Name	Name of the environment variable
Value	Value of variable

Set Environment Variables for Azure Web App Using Azure CLI

To set the same environment variables using Azure CLI, use the following Azure CLI command to add all the variables:

```
az webapp config appsettings set --resource-group
appsvc_windows_centralus_premium --name app-apress-asp
--settings AOAI_KEY="value" AOAI_ENDPOINT="value" AOAI_
DEPLOYMENTID="value"
```

Set Environment Variables for Azure Web App Using Azure PowerShell

To set the environment variables for Azure Web App using Azure PowerShell, you can use the following PowerShell script.

As you can see, doing the same task using Azure PowerShell takes a few extra lines when compared to Azure CLI.

To run the script, save the code as .PS1 and run.

```
# Retrieve current app settings
$app = Get-AzWebApp -ResourceGroupName "appsvc_windows_
centralus_premium" -Name "app-apress-asp"
$appSettings = $app.SiteConfig.AppSettings

# Add or update environment variables
$appSettings = @{ "AOAI_KEY"="value";"AOAI_
ENDPOINT"="value";"AOAI_DEPLOYMENTID"="value" }
# Update the app settings
Set-AzWebApp -ResourceGroupName "appsvc_windows_centralus_
premium" -Name "app-apress-asp" -AppSettings $appSettings
```

Test Application

Once the environment variables are set, we are ready to test the application. Click the Web App overview page, and click the Browse button, as shown in Figure 4-19.

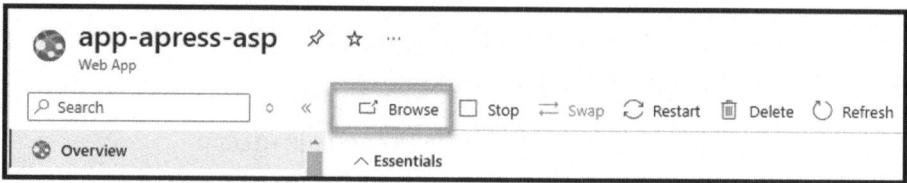

Figure 4-19. Browse

After clicking the Browse button, you should see the deployed application, as shown in Figure 4-20.

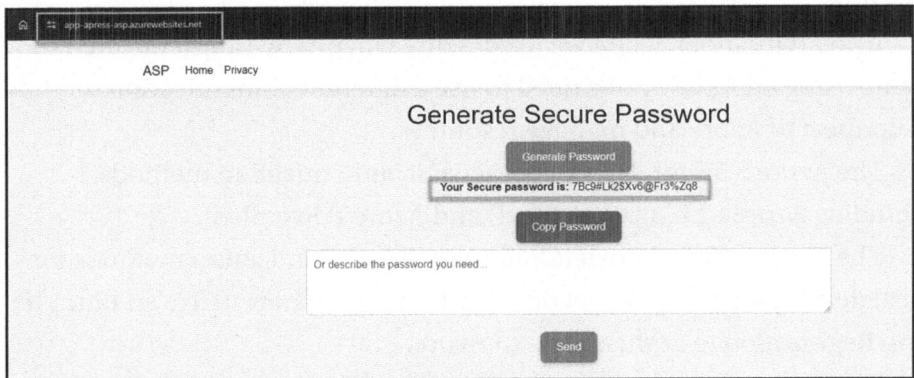

Figure 4-20. *Generate Secure Password page*

To test that the connection to Azure OpenAI is working, click the Generate Password button. You should see a password if the deployment was successful (Figure 4-20).

This part concludes the ASP.NET application setup and deployment. In the next section, we will build on our knowledge of the Azure .NET SDK and learn how to use the SDK with Azure's other resources.

Get Started with Azure OpenAI .NET SDK

Until now, we have been focused on learning how to use the Azure SDK for .NET with Azure OpenAI only. As mentioned in Chapter 1, Azure OpenAI is only a single library in the Azure SDK for .NET.

The SDK has more than 200 libraries that cover any Azure service and allow us to manage and deploy resources directly from a .NET application programmatically.

This section will show you how to use the SDK with Azure resources. You must first understand the authentication layer and how .NET connects to Azure.

If you remember, when we used Azure OpenAI, we authenticated to Azure using an API Key. We need to use a different authentication method to connect to Azure and manage resources.

The Azure SDK for .NET offers several authentication methods, including Azure CLI (az command) and Azure PowerShell.

The Azure CLI and PowerShell are good authentication methods for local development. In this section, I will show you how to use an Entra ID App Registration to authenticate to Azure.

Entra is Azure and Microsoft 365 underlining authentication service. Every time you log in to Azure, The Entra authentication service authorize your request.

An Entra App Registration is a like-a-service account (also known as a service principal) that has permissions to Azure in the form of role-based access control (RBAC).

RBAC permissions are based on a user role; for example, a database administrator will have permissions related to database management but not to virtual machine management.

When developing an application that will use Azure SDK for .NET, the authentication part is important, and you should spend a good portion of the time developing the right access policy and permission your application needs to have.

Create App Registration

We will start this process by creating an App Registration in Entra ID. Entra ID is a rebrand of the famous Azure Active Directory service. Entra now includes a suite of identity and access services, and Entra ID is one of them.

To create an App Registration, we will use Azure CLI.

Start with logging in to Azure using this command:

```
az login
```

This exercise will create an App Registration with Contributor permissions for the entire subscription.

Before you run the command, note down your subscription ID using this command:

```
az account show --query id --output tsv
```

After you have your subscription ID, run this command with your subscription ID:

```
az ad sp create-for-rbac -n AzureSDKService  --role Contributor --scopes /subscriptions/YOURSUBSCRIPTIONID
```

The command will create a service principal named AzureSDKService and assign it the Contributor permissions.

The command output will display the information we need to configure our application to authenticate to Azure. Note down the information.

```
{
"appId": "appid",
"displayName": "AzureSDKService",
"password": "password",
"tenant": "tenantID"
}
```

Create Environment Variables

To authenticate to Azure, we need to create the following environment variables:

- AZURE_CLIENT_ID

- AZURE_TENANT_ID

- AZURE_CLIENT_SECRET

Add the values from the output to the following commands and inside a VS Code terminal.

```
$env:AZURE_CLIENT_ID="APP ID"
$env:AZURE_TENANT_ID="Tenant ID "
$env:AZURE_CLIENT_SECRET="Password "
```

To check if the environment variables are set correctly, run this command:

```
Get-ChildItem -Path Env:\AZURE_*
```

If you can see the new variables in the command output, you're ready to move to the next section.

Create C# Console Application for Azure Resources

At this stage, we are ready to go ahead and create a C# Console application that receives information from Azure.

Start with creating a C# Console application using this command:

```
dotnet new console
```

Note   If you started a new VS Code editor, please make sure you set
the environment variables.

In our exercise, we will use the SDK to display the details of a resource
group called Apress and list all the Azure AI service accounts in a single
resource group.

Install Packages

To view our resources and connect to Azure, run the commands below to
install the packages that will help us achieve our goal:

```
dotnet add package Azure.Identity --version 1.11.3
dotnet add package Azure.ResourceManager --version 1.12.0
dotnet add package Microsoft.Extensions.Azure --version 1.7.3
```

Code: Program.cs

After you install the packages, copy the following code to your Program.cs
file. The code has the following main stages:

- Authenticate to Azure using the ArcClient class, and
  use the environment variables we set.

- Use the default Azure subscription.

- Retrieve the details of all the resource groups in the
  subscription.

- Show the details of a resource group called OpenAI.

- Show all the Azure AI accounts inside the OpenAI
  resource group.

```
using System;
using System.Threading.Tasks;
using Azure.Core;
using Azure.Identity;
using Azure.ResourceManager;
using Azure.ResourceManager.Resources;
using Azure;

class Program
{
    static async Task Main(string[] args)
    {
        // Create an instance of ArmClient using Default
        AzureCredential
        ArmClient armClient = new ArmClient(new DefaultAzure
        Credential());

        // Get the default Azure subscription
        var subdetails = armClient.GetDefaultSubscription();
        Console.WriteLine($"The default Azure subscription
        is: {subdetails.Id}");

        // Get all resource groups in the subscription
        ResourceGroupCollection resourceGroupCollection =
        subdetails.GetResourceGroups();

        // Iterate over the resource group collection
        await foreach (var resourceGroup in
        resourceGroupCollection.GetAllAsync())
        {
            if (resourceGroup.Data.Name == "OpenAI")
            {
```

```
        Console.WriteLine($"Resource Group ID:
        {resourceGroup.Id}");
        Console.WriteLine($"Resource Group Name:
        {resourceGroup.Data.Name}");
        Console.WriteLine($"Resource Group Location:
        {resourceGroup.Data.Location}");
        Console.WriteLine("-----------
        ------------------------------");
    }
}

// Get generic resources with specific filter and
expand properties
AsyncPageable<GenericResource> networkAndVmWith
TestInName = subdetails.GetGenericResourcesAsync(
    // Set filter to only return virtual network and
    virtual machine resource with 'test' in the name
    filter: "(resourceType eq 'Microsoft.Cognitive
    Services/accounts') and substringof('OpenAI',
    resourceGroup) ",
    // Include 'createdTime' and 'changeTime'
    properties in the returned data
    expand: "createdTime,changedTime"
);

int count = 0;
await foreach (var res in networkAndVmWithTestInName)
{
    Console.WriteLine($"{res.Id.Name} in resource group
    {res.Id.ResourceGroupName} created at {res.Data.
    CreatedOn} and changed at {res.Data.ChangedOn}");
    count++;
```

```
        }
        Console.WriteLine($"{count} resources found");
    }
}
```

Note   In line 27, you need to specify an Azure Resource group.

To run the application, open a terminal session in the root folder of the application and run this command:

```
dotnet run
```

The output will show the default Azure subscription and the number of Azure OpenAI resources in a Resource Group called OpenAI.

```
The default Azure subscription is: /subscriptions/
subscriptionID
2 resources found
```

This code is a simple example showing how powerful Azure SDK is for .NET. With the SDK we can target any Azure Service using a library that exposes the service to .NET.

Azure OpenAI On Your Data

Up until now, we have used Azure OpenAI with what is known as a public data set. The LLM's knowledge was based on public information available on the Internet.

But what if you would like to create an AI application grounded in enterprise data? Or a specific data set?

Azure OpenAI allows us to use AI models on our data. With this feature, any interaction with the model is done on top of the data we provided the model with.

In this exercise, we will use Azure OpenAI Studio to create a chat application that runs on top of provided data.

When we chat with the model, it will only provide answers from the data we loaded. In the example we use a C# cheat sheet file and ask the model to provide answers from the file.

Azure OpenAI On Your Data is available via the SDK, REST API, and as you will see from Azure OpenAI Studio.

To get started, Open the Azure OpenAI Studio using the following URL `https://oai.azure.com/`.

Remember to switch to your Azure OpenAI resource from the top right corner.

Make sure you have a GPT-4 model deployed before starting.

From the Azure OpenAI portal, click Chat (Figure 4-21).

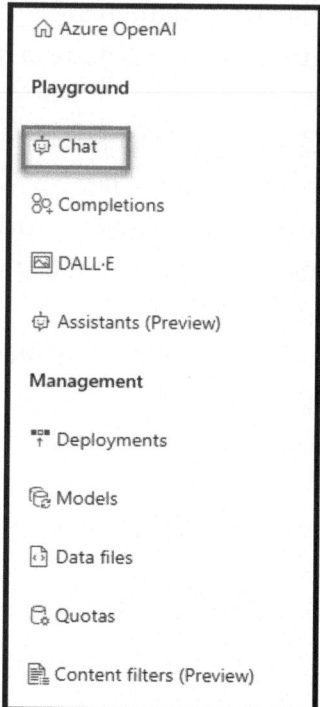

Figure 4-21. *Chat*

Create Blob Storage

From the setup page, click Add your data, as shown in Figure 4-22.

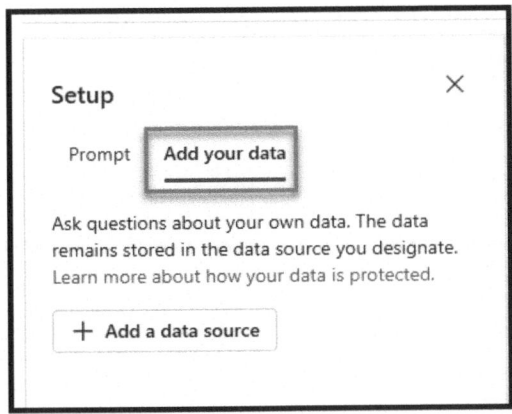

Figure 4-22. *Add your data*

Click + Add a data source.

The selected data source windows allow us to select data sources from several locations. In our case, we will use the Upload files (Preview) option.

Select your subscription from the list if you have more than one.

In Select Azure Blob Storage Resource, Click Create a new Azure Blob storage resource, as shown in Figure 4-23.

Add data

● Data source	**Select or add data source**
	Your data source is used to ground the generated results with your data. Select an existing data source or create a new dat
○ Upload files	connection with Azure Blob Storage, databases, search, URLs, or local files as the source the grounding data will be built fr
	Learn more about data privacy and security in Azure AI. ☐
○ Data management	**Select data source ***
	Upload files (preview) ⌄
○ Review and finish	**Subscription ***
	Pay-As-You-Go ⌄
	Select Azure Blob storage resource ⓘ *****
	cs11003bffd9e44e271 ⌄ ↻
	Create a new Azure Blob storage resource ☐

Figure 4-23. *Add data*

From the Create Blob storage resource, configure the account with the following settings (Figure 4-24):

- Standard storage tier

- Locally redundant storage (LRS)

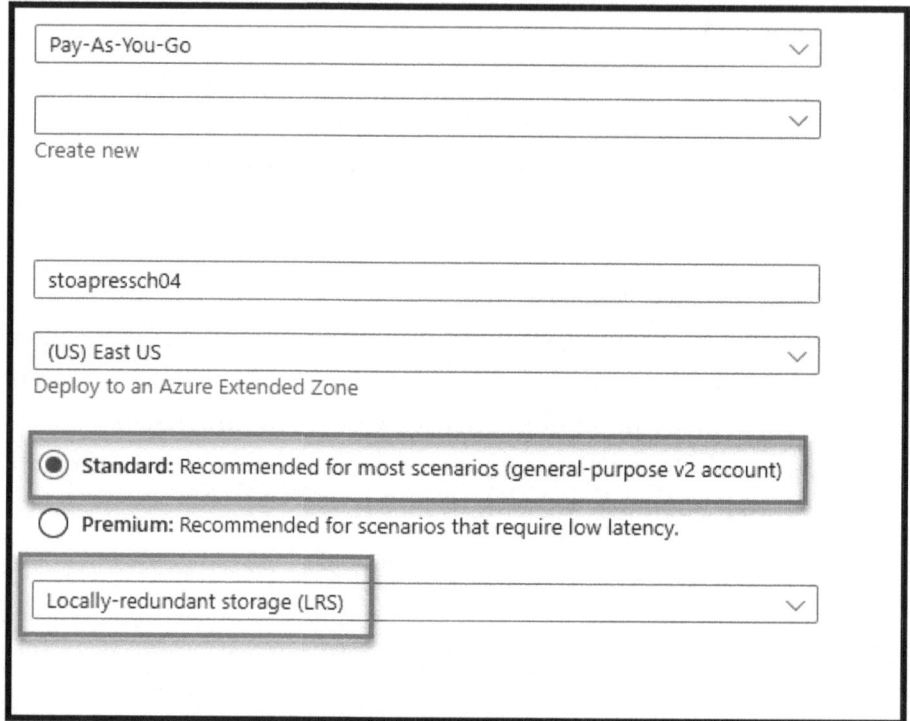

Figure 4-24. *Storage account*

After creating the account, refresh the Select Azure blob storage dropdown box.

Enable CORS

Before continuing to search configuration, make sure you click the Turn on CORS button, as shown in Figure 4-25.

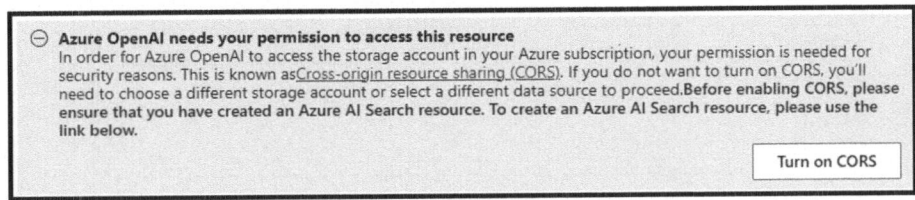

Figure 4-25. *Enable CORS on the Storage account*

Enable Azure AI Search

After enabling CORS, we need to create an Azure AI Search resource. A search resource will index the content of our data and enable the AI model to answer questions regarding the data.

To enable Azure AI Search resource, click Create a new Azure Resource, as shown in Figure 4-26.

Figure 4-26. *Azure AI search*

In the Create Azure AI Search page, fill in the search name and select the pricing tier (Figure 4-27). I'm selecting the Basic service tier for this exercise.

Note   Azure AI Search is an expensive service. Make sure you delete it after you finish this lab.

After the deployment is complete, review the Add data windows and make sure all the necessary services are enabled.

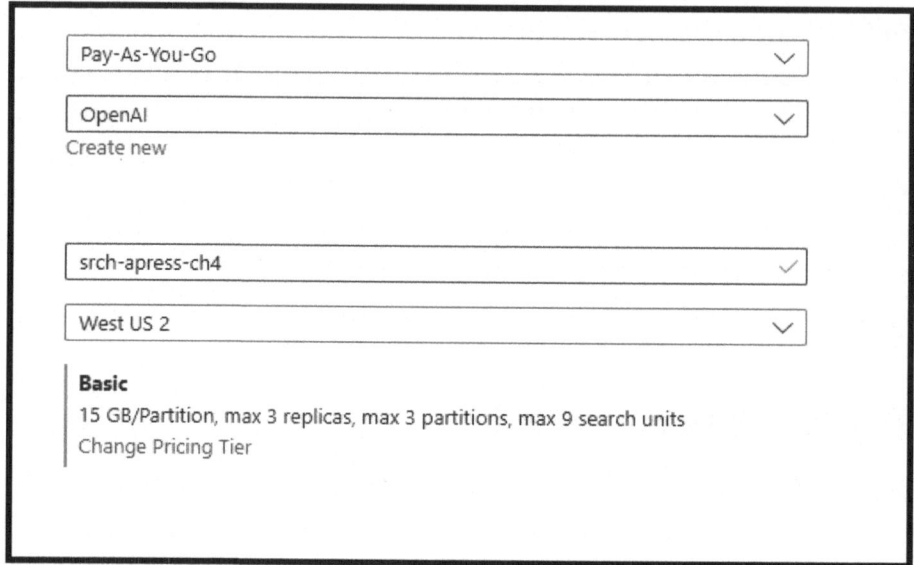

Figure 4-27. *Create Azure AI Search resource*

In the Index name, type Default, as shown in Figure 4-28.

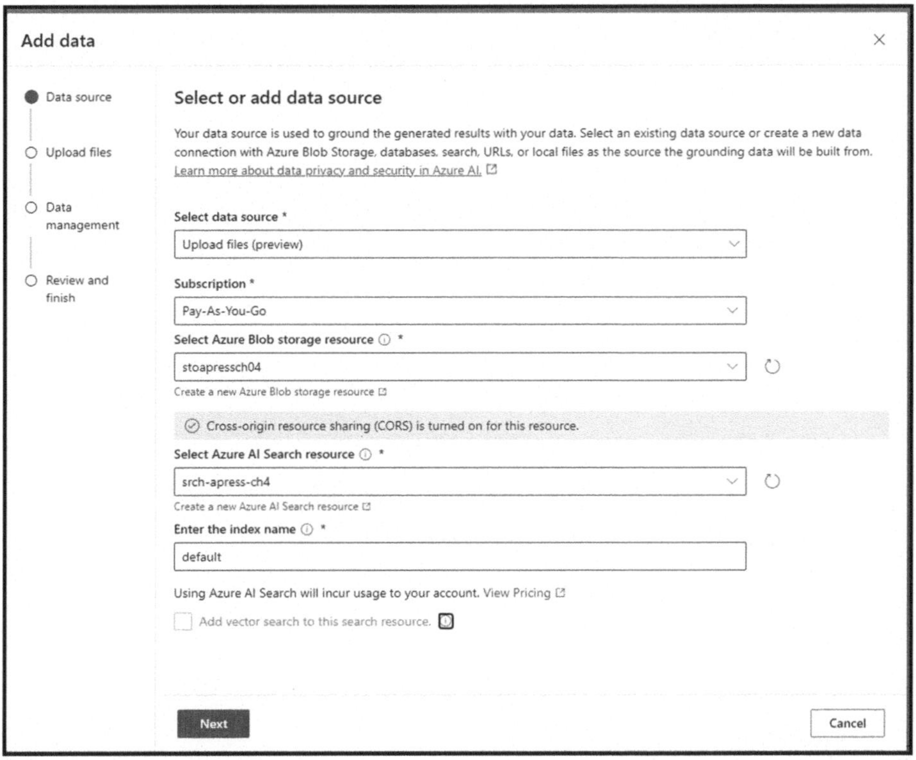

Figure 4-28. *Add data*

Click Next to continue.

Add PDF File

For this exercise, I have prepared a C# Cheat Sheet PDF file (you will find it in the Repo of this book).

From the Upload files screen, click Browse for a file and select the PDF file.

Figure 4-29 shows parts of the PDF file.

```
C# Cheat Sheet


Basics
- Variable Declaration:
  int age = 30;
  string name = "John";
  bool isActive = true;


- Data Types:
  - Value Types: int, float, double, decimal, bool, char, byte, short, long, struct, enum
  - Reference Types: string, array, class, interface, delegate


- Control Structures:
  // if-else
  if (condition) { }
  else if (condition) { }
  else { }
```

Figure 4-29. *PDF file*

After you upload the file successfully, upload and click Next
(Figure 4-30).

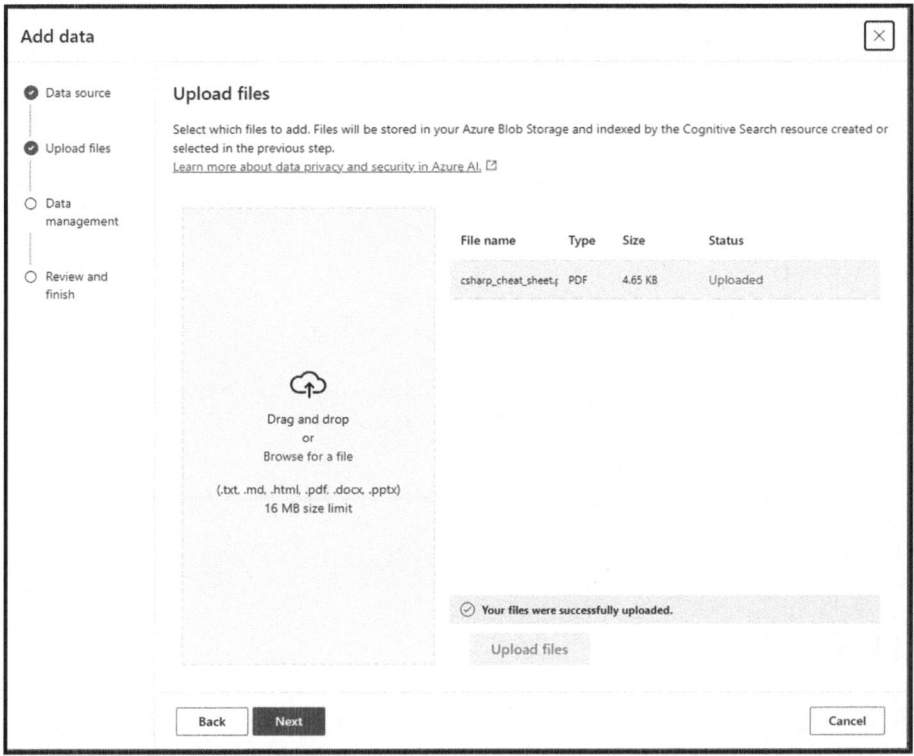

Figure 4-30.   *Upload files*

Leave the data management options with the default settings and click next to finish the process.

You can monitor the indexing progress from the add your data tab, as shown in Figure 4-31.

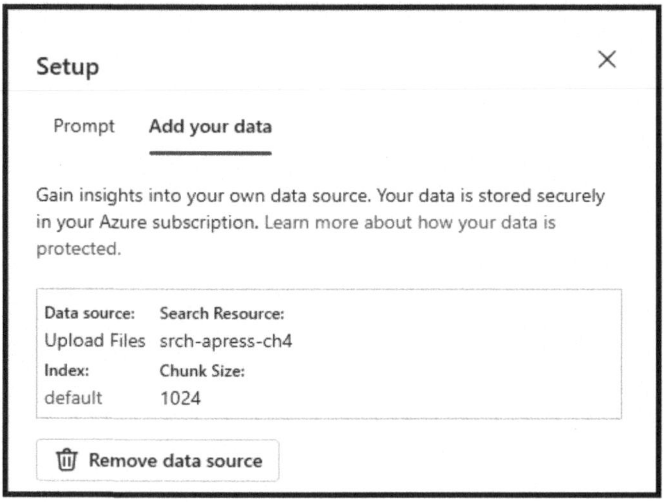

Setup   ×

   Prompt   **Add your data**
              ─────────────

Gain insights into your own data source. Your data is stored securely
in your Azure subscription. Learn more about how your data is
protected.

Data source:	Search Resource:
Upload Files	srch-apress-ch4
Index:	Chunk Size:
default	1024

🗑 Remove data source

Figure 4-31. *Upload status*

Ask Questions

We are ready to ask the AI model questions about our data at this stage.
Remember, this is just a small example. In real-use cases, the data source
can be a database and dynamic content that updates in real time.

In the System message screen (Figure 4-32), add a system message. In
my case, I added the following:

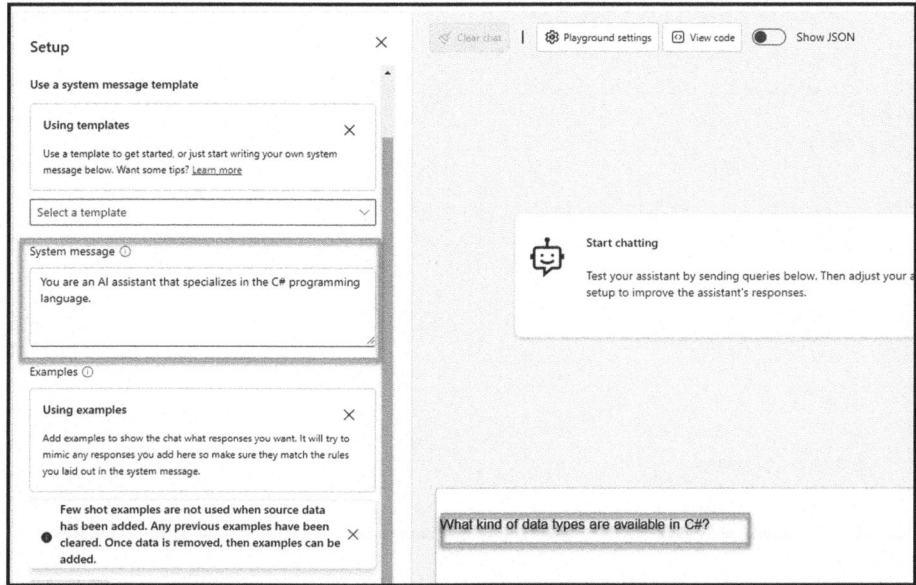

Figure 4-32. *Chat windows*

You are an AI assistant that specializes in C# programming language.

In the chat window, ask the model a question about the data. In my case, I asked the following question:

What kind of data types are available in C#?

You can see the answer from the model in Figure 4-33.

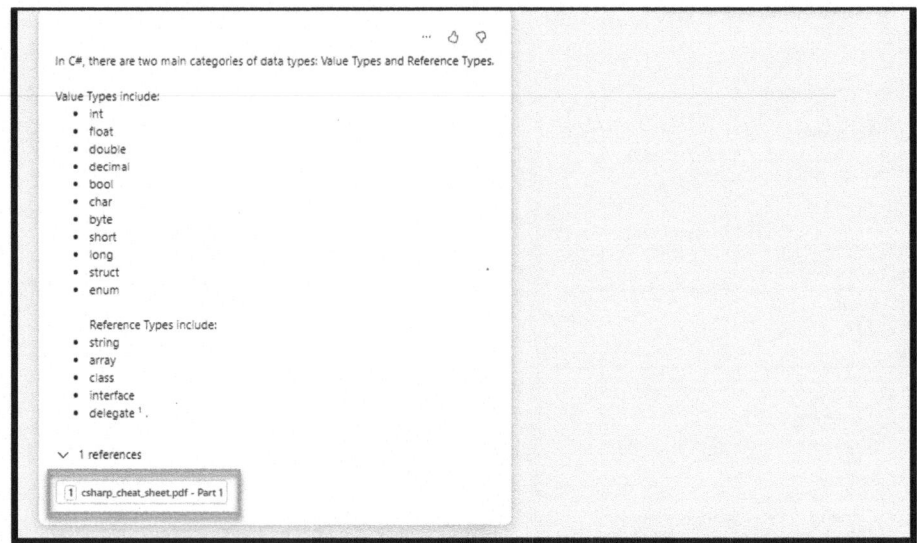

Figure 4-33. *Returned answer from the model*

Figure 4-34 shows another example of how I asked the model about loops in C#.

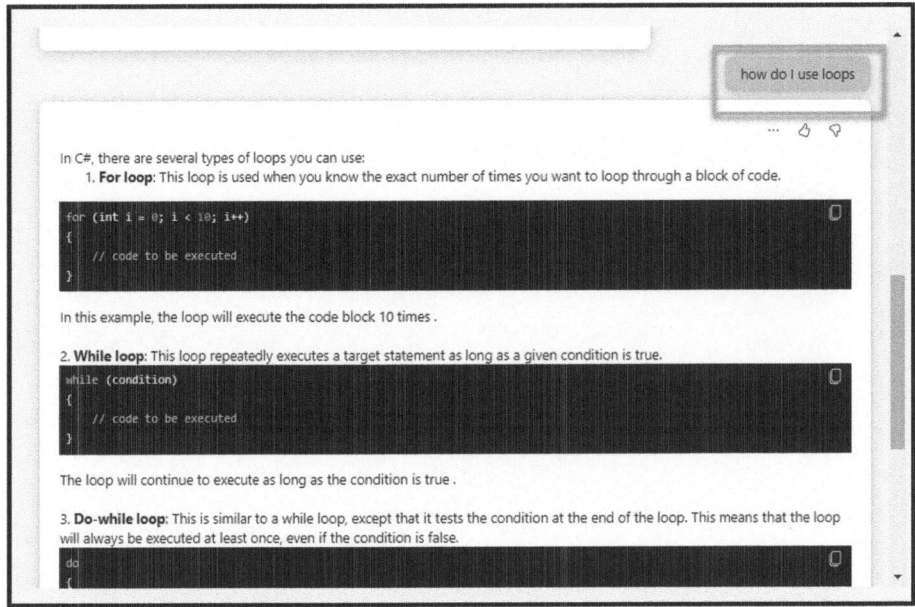

Figure 4-34. *C# loops*

Chapter Summary

In this chapter, we learned how to use ASP.NET applications with Azure OpenAI and create an app that generates secure passwords using a GPT-4 AI model. We also deployed the application to Azure Web App.

We also learned how to use the Azure SDK for .NET to list resources using a C# Console application.

In the book's final section, we created a chat application in Azure OpenAI Studio that uses our data using Azure OpenAI On Your Data.

CHAPTER 5

Introduction to Assistants

In this chapter, we will focus on the Azure OpenAI Assistants API. We discuss this API briefly in Chapter 1, and in this chapter, we will dive deeper into the topic and learn how to use it.

Assistants API

The Assistants API offers new capabilities that allow developers to build advanced and powerful AI assistants that are not limited to creating content and providing information.

With the Assistants API, we can build AI assistants that can

- Access tools like file search and code interpreter hosted by OpenAI or custom-build tools hosted externally.

- Access persistent threads and the capability to store message history. The new API takes care of truncating the conversation history and reduces it if it is too long.

© The Editor(s) (if applicable) and The Author(s),
under exclusive license to APress Media, LLC, part of Springer Nature 2024
S. Ifrah, *Getting Started with Azure OpenAI*, https://doi.org/10.1007/979-8-8688-0599-8_5

Assistants API Objects and Components

The Assistants API uses the following multiple components and objects to deliver the new capabilities.

Component	Details
Assistant	The AI that uses Azure OpenAI models and tools
Thread	The persistent conversation history between an Assistant and a user. The history is managed automatically by the Assistant
Message	Any message created by an Assistant or a user and can include text, images or files (stored as a list)
Run	Task and activation of an Assistant on a message or thread
Run step	List of steps an Assistant took as part of a Run

Context Windows

If you remember, from Chapter 1, we discuss the concept of a Context Window and how we are limited by the number of tokens we can send and receive from a model.

With the Assistants API, Context Window management is handled by the API.

The Assistants automatically truncate text to ensure we stay within the model's context window length limits.

In addition to the API management of the Context Window, we can also control token usage per run using the following parameters.

Parameter	Details
max_prompt_tokens	Control token usage in a single run
max_completion_tokens	Control token usage in a single run

Create AI Assistants Using C#

In this section, we will create a C# Console application that uses the Assistants API. As you will see shortly, the process of creating an AI assistant application is a bit different compared to the C# console application we created in Chapter 3.

In this exercise, we will create an AI coding assistant that will answer a coding question. This is just a simple example, but you can easily add a prompt and make it more advanced.

Create Azure OpenAI Resource and Deployment Using Azure CLI

Before we get into the code of the Assistants SDK, let's go ahead and deploy an Azure OpenAI Resource and Deployment using Azure CLI.

Note   To access the Assistants API, we need to deploy a Preview model (gpt-4-1106-Preview).

To create an Azure OpenAI resource and deploy a model. Let's start by logging in to Azure using the following Azure CLI command:

```
az login
```

After login, we can run the following lines of code that will do the following:

- Create an Azure Resource Group in the EastUS region.

- Create an Azure OpenAI resource named aoi-apress-ai.

- Create an Azure OpenAI deployment using GPT-4 model (gpt-4-1106-Preview).

```
# Create an Azure resource group

az group create --name rg-apress-ai --location eastus

# Create an Azure OpenAI resource

az cognitiveservices account create  --name aoi-apress-ai
--location eastus --resource-group rg-apress-ai --kind OpenAI
--sku S0

# Create an Azure OpenAI deployment
az cognitiveservices account deployment create --name aoi-
apress-ai --resource-group rg-apress-ai --deployment-name gpt-4
--model-name gpt-4-1106-Preview  --model-format OpenAI --model-
version 0613   --sku-name "Standard" --sku-capacity "1"
```

Create Console Application

To create a Console application using C#, open VS Code.

Open the terminal window in VS Code and create a directory.

```
mkdir Chapter-5
cd Chapter-5
mkdir assistants
dotnet new console
```

The above commands will create a C# Console application called Assistants in a directory called Chapter 5.

Install Package

To use the Assistants API, we need to install the following NuGet package (Figure 5-1): www.nuget.org/packages/Azure.AI.OpenAI. Assistants/1.0.0-beta.4

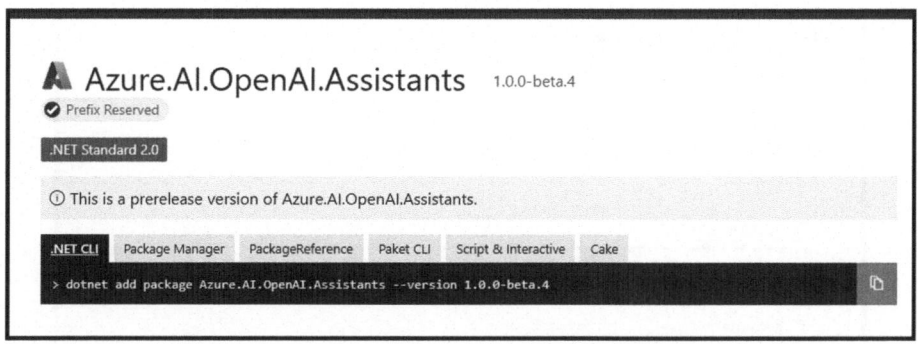

Figure 5-1. *Azure OpenAI Assistants package*

From the VS Code terminal window, run the following command to install the package:

```
dotnet add package Azure.AI.OpenAI.Assistants --version
1.0.0-beta.4
```

Set Environment Variables

To access the Azure OpenAI resource and deployment, we need to set the following environment variables.

From the VS Code terminal window, run the following commands:

```
$env:AOAI_KEY="API Key"
$env:AOAI_ENDPOINT="Azure OpenAI resource End Point URL "
```

Note   We will add the deployment name to the actual code of the application.

Before you move to the next step, please make sure the deployed model name is gpt-4-1106-Preview (Figure 5-2).

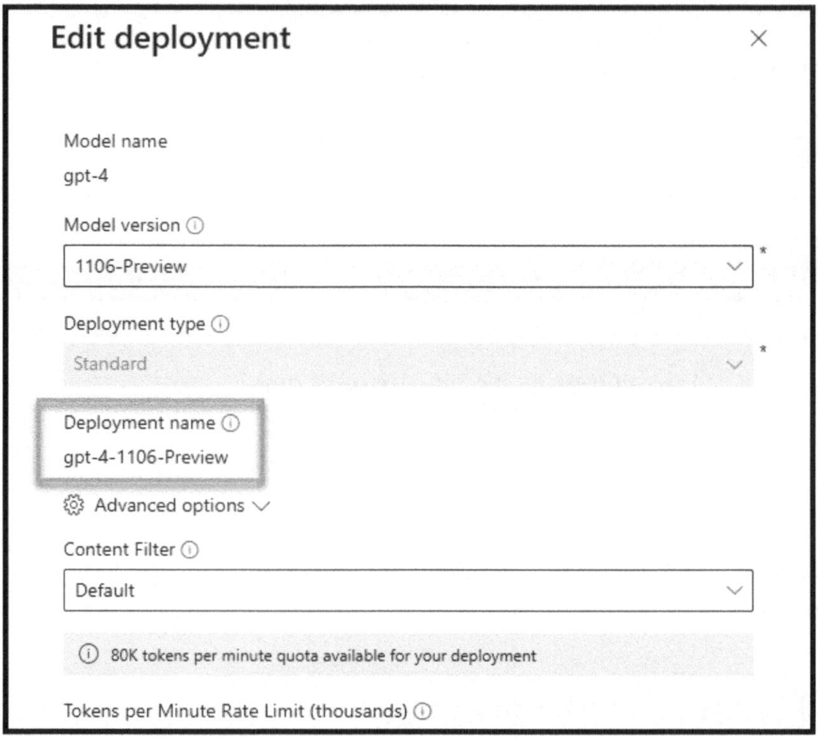

Figure 5-2. *Deployment details*

You will find it in the Azure OpenAI portal on the Deployments page.

Note   You will find the code for this exercise in the book's repository.

Program.cs

Now that you have the environment variables set, open the Program.cs file inside your Console application, and add the following code that will create an AI Assistant.

The code will do the following:

1. Import the Azure.AI.OpenAI.Assistants namespace.

2. Load the environment variables.

3. Create an Assistant using the Assistant class library.

4. Set the assistant class.

5. Create a thread and add a question.

6. Run the thread.

7. Provide an answer.

```
using Azure; // Import the Azure namespace
using Azure.AI.OpenAI.Assistants; // Import the Azure.
AI.OpenAI.Assistants namespace

string endpoint = Environment.GetEnvironmentVariable("AOAI_
ENDPOINT") ?? throw new ArgumentNullException("AOAI_ENDPOINT");
// Get the endpoint from environment variables or throw an
exception if it's null
string key = Environment.GetEnvironmentVariable("AOAI_KEY") ??
throw new ArgumentNullException("AOAI_KEY"); // Get the key
from environment variables or throw an exception if it's null
AssistantsClient client = new AssistantsClient(new
Uri(endpoint), new AzureKeyCredential(key)); // Create a new
instance of AssistantsClient using the endpoint and key

// Create an assistant
Assistant assistant = await client.CreateAssistantAsync(
    new AssistantCreationOptions("gpt-4-1106-Preview")
    // Replace this with the name of your model deployment
    {
        Name = "Code Assistant", // Set the name of the
                                   assistant
```

```
        Instructions = "You are a knowledgeable coding
        assistant. Write and run code to solve programming-
        related questions.", // Set the instructions for the
                          assistant
        Tools = { new CodeInterpreterToolDefinition() }
// Add a code interpreter tool definition
    });

// Create a thread
AssistantThread thread = await client.CreateThreadAsync();

// Add a user question to the thread
ThreadMessage message = await client.CreateMessageAsync(
    thread.Id,
    MessageRole.User,
    "I need to write a function in C# that reverses a string.
    Can you help me??"); // Create a user message with the
                      question

// Run the thread
ThreadRun run = await client.CreateRunAsync(
    thread.Id,
    new CreateRunOptions(assistant.Id)
);

// Wait for the assistant to respond
do
{
    await Task.Delay(TimeSpan.FromMilliseconds(300));
    // Delay for 300 milliseconds
    run = await client.GetRunAsync(thread.Id, run.Id);
    // Get the status of the run
}
```

```csharp
while (run.Status == RunStatus.Queued
    || run.Status == RunStatus.InProgress); // Continue looping
    while the run is queued or in progress

// Get the messages
PageableList<ThreadMessage> messagesPage = await client.
GetMessagesAsync(thread.Id); // Get the messages for the thread
IReadOnlyList<ThreadMessage> messages = messagesPage.Data;
// Get the data from the messages page

foreach (ThreadMessage threadMessage in messages.Reverse())
// Iterate over the messages in reverse order
{
    Console.Write($"{threadMessage.CreatedAt:yyyy-MM-dd
    HH:mm:ss} - {threadMessage.Role,10}: ");
    // Print the timestamp and role of the message
    foreach (MessageContent contentItem in threadMessage.
    ContentItems) // Iterate over the content items in
                    the message
    {
        if (contentItem is MessageTextContent textItem)
        // Check if the content item is of type
        MessageTextContent
        {
            Console.Write(textItem.Text);
            // Print the text content
        }
        Console.WriteLine(); // Print a new line
    }
}
```

Run Application

To run the application, use the following command:

dotnet run

The output of the application should look like:

> 2024-06-03 01:51:44 - user: I need to write a function in C# that reverses a string. Can you help me??

> 2024-06-03 01:51:46 - assistant: Certainly! Below is a simple C# function that takes a string as an input and returns its reverse.

```csharp
using System;

public class StringReverser
{
    public static string ReverseString(string s)
    {
        char[] charArray = s.ToCharArray();
        Array.Reverse(charArray);
        return new string(charArray);
    }

    public static void Main(string[] args)
    {
        string originalString = "Hello, World!";
        string reversedString = ReverseString(originalString);
    }
}
```

To use the above code:

1. Copy the code into a C# environment or file.

2. Compile and run the program.

I cannot run C# code in this environment because it's set up for Python. However, the provided function should work in any C# development environment such as Visual Studio, Visual Studio Code with the C# extension, or an online C# compiler.

As you can see from the above output, the outcome is detailed and specific. If the request was to generate a Python code, the API could test the program using the code_interpreter tool and test the code before.

Create AI Assistants Using Postman

In this section we will learn how to use the AI Assistants API with Postman. As I said earlier, the Assistants API has many advantages over the chat API. These advantages also require us to take extra steps when interacting with an assistant.

As you will see in this section, to ask the Assistance API a question and retrieve the answer, we need to use five API requests. These steps involve the following.

Step	Details
1	Create an Assistant
2	Create a thread
3	Add a user question to a thread
4	Run thread
5	Retrieve assistant response

As you can see in the table, interacting with the Assistant API a bit of planning. The reason we need to take the extra steps is because of the advanced features the API offers, like code interpreter and, most importantly, the persistent chat.

The above steps also match the components the API has, and each step targets one of the components.

Figure 5-3 shows the five REST API requests we will use in Postman to interact with an Assistant.

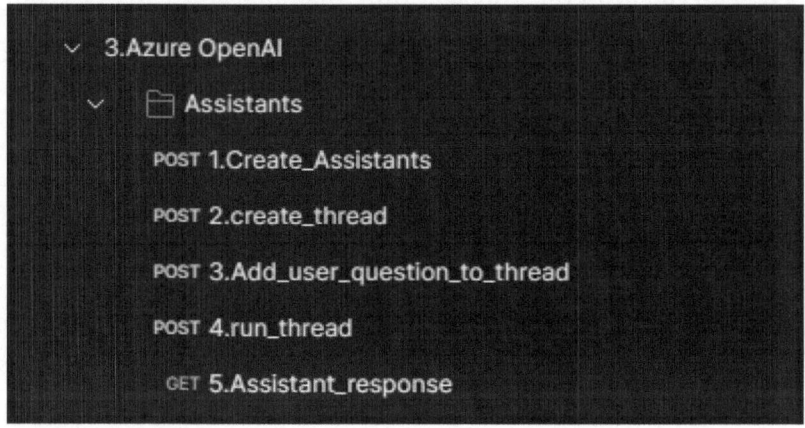

Figure 5-3. *Assistants API requests*

Note   Please review Chapter 2 for more details on setting up Postman with Azure OpenAI.

This exercise will create the same coding assistance we created in the previous section.

Create an Assistant

To create an assistant, we will start by creating a POST request.

In Postman, the following POST request.

Request type	POST
URL	{{ENDPOINTURL}}//openai/assistants?api-version=2024-05-01-preview

Body	{
	"instructions": "You are a knowledgeable coding assistant. Write and run code to solve programming-
	related questions.",
	"name": "Code Assistant",
	"tools": [{"type": "code_interpreter"}],
	"model": "gpt-4-1106-preview"
	}

Auth Type	API Key Key = api-key Value = Use API Key from Azure OpenAI Resource Please see Figure 5-6

Note   In this request, I'm using API Version 2024-05-1. To check the latest API version, visit https://learn.microsoft.com/en-us/azure/ai-services/openai/how-to/assistant.

Your request should look like Figure 5-4.

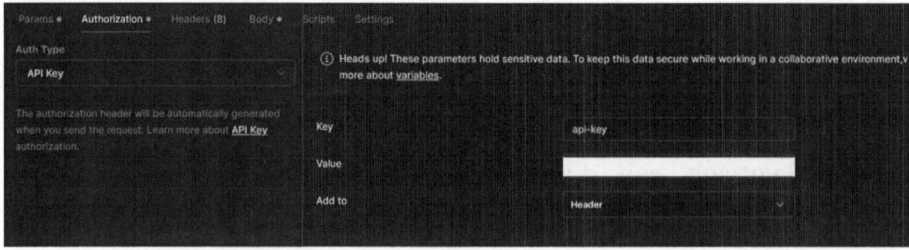

Figure 5-4. *POST Request*

The body tab should look like Figure 5-5.

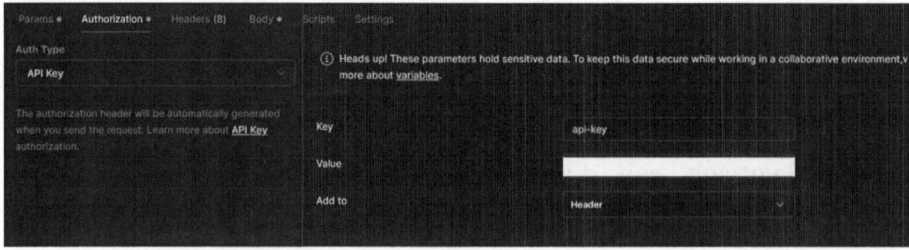

Figure 5-5. *POST Request*

The Authorization request should look like Figure 5-6. Make sure you use the API Key from your Azure OpenAI resource.

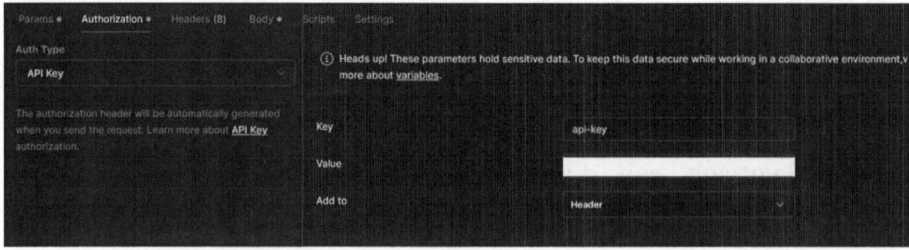

Figure 5-6. *API Key*

Save the request and click on Send to create an Assistant. The output from the request will be an Assistant object that looks like:

Take note of the id value. The id value contains the id of the assistant object, and we will use it soon.

```
{
    "id": "asst_A8aZAbmJGZTaZLr46Do2G6I6",
    "object": "assistant",
    "created_at": 1717391587,
    "name": "Code Assistant",
    "description": null,
    "model": "gpt-4-1106-preview",
    "instructions": "You are a knowledgeable coding assistant.
    Write and run code to solve programming-related
    questions.",
    "tools": [
        {
            "type": "code_interpreter"
        }
    ],
    "top_p": 1.0,
    "temperature": 1.0,
    "tool_resources": {
        "code_interpreter": {
            "file_ids": []
        }
    },
    "metadata": {},
    "response_format": "auto"
}
```

Create Thread

After creating an Assistant, it is time to create a thread. To create a thread, we will create the following POST request. In this request, there is no Body as shown in Figure 5-7.

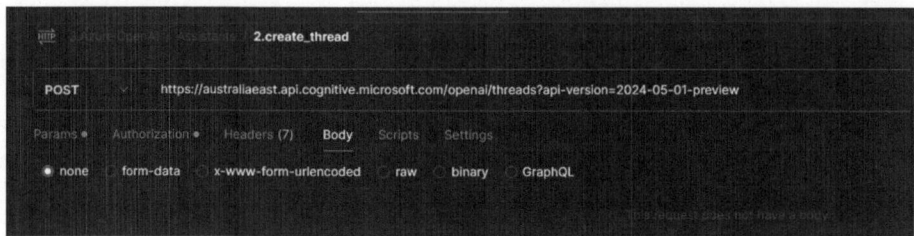

Figure 5-7. *Create Thread*

Please use the following table to create the thread.

Request type	POST
URL	{{ENDPOINTURL}}/openai/threads?api-version=2024-05-01-preview
Body	
Auth Type	API Key Key = api-key Value = Use API Key from Azure OpenAI Resource Please see Figure 5-6

The output of this request will contain an object with a thread id. Note it down, as we will need it soon. The returned object should look like this.

```
{
    "id": "thread_8iSGbfJENTy6zNbFBPxC7TYd",
    "object": "thread",
    "created_at": 1717391631,
    "metadata": {},
    "tool_resources": {}
}
```

Add User Question to Thread

Now, we will create a message containing our question for the assistant. In Postman, create another POST request with the details shown in the table. Figure 5-8 shows the POST request.

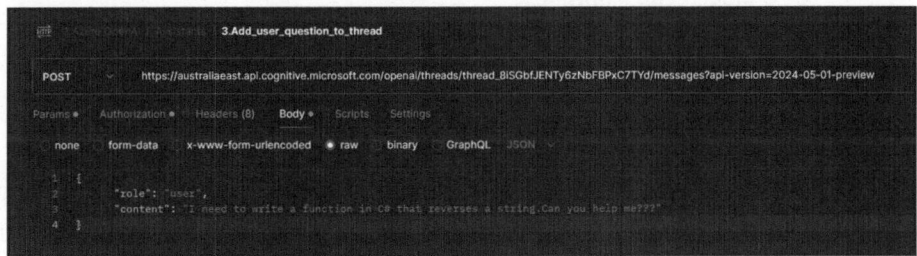

Figure 5-8. *Add user question to thread*

Use the following table to create the request. Make sure you add your thread id.

Request type	POST
URL	`{{ENDPOINTURL}}/openai/threads/{{THREAD ID}}` `/messages?api-version=2024-05-01-preview`
Body	`{` `"role": "user",` `"content": "I need to write a function in C# that reverses a string. Can you help me???"` `}`
Auth Type	API Key Key = api-key Value = Use API Key from Azure OpenAI Resource Please see Figure 5-6

Run Thread

We have an Assistant, a Thread, and a question at this stage. The only thing left is to submit the question to the assistant. Let's create a request that will run the thread.

Create a POST request in Postman, including the thread id in the URL and assistant id in the body as listed in the following table and in Figure 5-9.

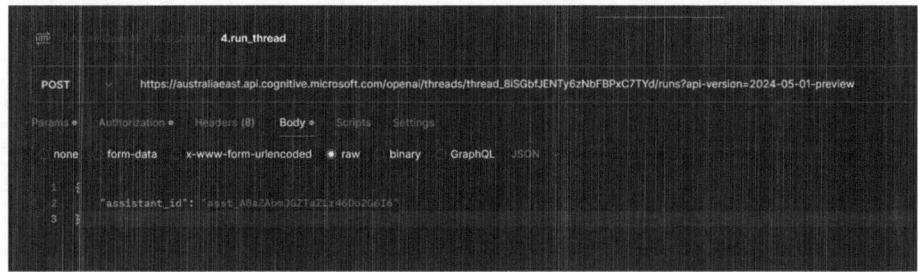

Figure 5-9. *Run thread*

The following table shows details of the run thread request.

Request type	POST
URL	{{ENDPOINTURL}}/openai/threads/{{THREAD ID}} /runs?api-version=2024-05-01-preview

Body	{
	"assistant_id": "{{ASSISTANT ID}} "
	}

Auth Type	API Key Key = api-key Value = Use API Key from Azure OpenAI Resource Please see Figure 5-6

Once we send the request, the only thing left to do is retrieve the request from the assistant.

Assistant Response

To retrieve the response from the Assistant, create a GET request in
Postman with the following details (shown in Figure 5-10 and in the table).
This request also includes the thread ID in the URL and the assistant ID in
the body.

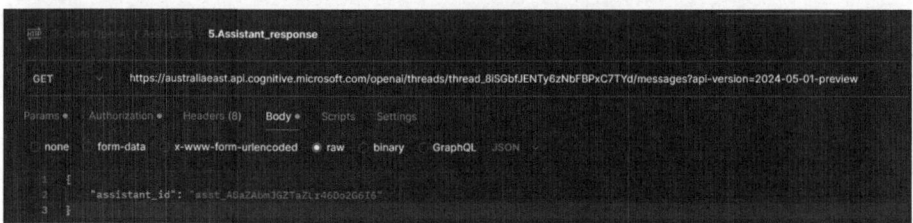

Figure 5-10. *Assistant response*

The following table shows the GET request details.

Request type	GET
URL	{{ENDPOINTURL}}/openai/threads/{{THREAD ID}}/ messages?api-version=2024-05-01-preview

Body	{
	"assistant_id": "{{ASSISTANT ID}} "
	}

Auth Type	API Key Key = api-key Value = Use API Key from Azure OpenAI Resource Please see Figure 5-6

The response body should look like this:

```
{
    "object": "list",
    "data": [
        {
            "id": "msg_OePkuUxDgZRdXUnarwVj31HI",
            "object": "thread.message",
            "created_at": 1717391797,
            "assistant_id": "asst_A8aZAbmJGZTaZLr46Do2G6I6",
            "thread_id": "thread_8iSGbfJENTy6zNbFBPxC7TYd",
            "run_id": "run_LYogfvTvaefzs8o69XFGuroy",
            "role": "assistant",
            "content": [
                {
                    "type": "text",
                    "text": {
                        "value": "Certainly! Here's a
                        simple C# function that takes a
                        string as input and returns its
                        reverse:\n\n```csharp\npublic
                        static string ReverseString(string
                        input)\n{\n    if (string.
                        IsNullOrEmpty(input))\n        return
                        input;\n\n    char[] array =
                        input.ToCharArray();\n    Array.
                        Reverse(array);\n    return new
                        string(array);\n}\n```\n\nYou can call
                        this function with a string argument,
                        and it will return the reversed
                        string. Here's how you'd use the
                        function:\n\n```csharp\nstring original
```

```
                    = \"Hello, World!\";\nstring reversed
                    = ReverseString(original);\nConsole.
                    WriteLine(\"Reversed string: \" +
                    reversed);\n```\n\nWhen you run this
                    piece of code, it will output:\n\n```\
                    nReversed string: !dlroW ,olleH\n```\n\
                    nIf you need help with anything else,
                    such as how to compile and run the
                    code, let me know!",
                    "annotations": []
              }
          }
      ],
      "attachments": [],
      "metadata": {}
  },
  {
      "id": "msg_Ohk2ZoERxOsnSzmekKtLjxgJ",
      "object": "thread.message",
      "created_at": 1717391683,
      "assistant_id": null,
      "thread_id": "thread_8iSGbfJENTy6zNbFBPxC7TYd",
      "run_id": null,
      "role": "user",
      "content": [
          {
              "type": "text",
              "text": {
                  "value": "I need to write a function
                  in C# that reverses a string.Can you
                  help me???",
```

```
                    "annotations": []
                }
            }
        ],
        "attachments": [],
        "metadata": {}
    }
],
"first_id": "msg_OePkuUxDgZRdXUnarwVj31HI",
"last_id": "msg_Ohk2ZoERxOsnSzmekKtLjxgJ",
"has_more": false
}
```

As you saw, using the Assistants API with Postman and C# requires a few steps. Make sure you understand the components in play and the order in which they work.

You can read more about the Assistants API in the following URL:

```
https://platform.openai.com/docs/assistants/how-it-works
```

Use Azure OpenAI Text to Speech with Postman

As mentioned in Chapter 1, Azure OpenAI offers a range of AI models from OpenAI. One of them is the text-to-speech model that allows us to send text to an AI model and convert it into voice in real time.

Many applications and use cases can leverage this feature, and in this section, we will learn how to use the Azure OpenAI text-to-speech service.

Since this service is currently available using REST API, we will use the Postman API client.

Create a Resource and Deployment

Since the text-to-speech model service is being enroll, it is currently
available in two regions only, North Central United States and
Sweden North.

In Figure 5-11, you can see a text-to-speech model (tts) when selecting
a North Central US region.

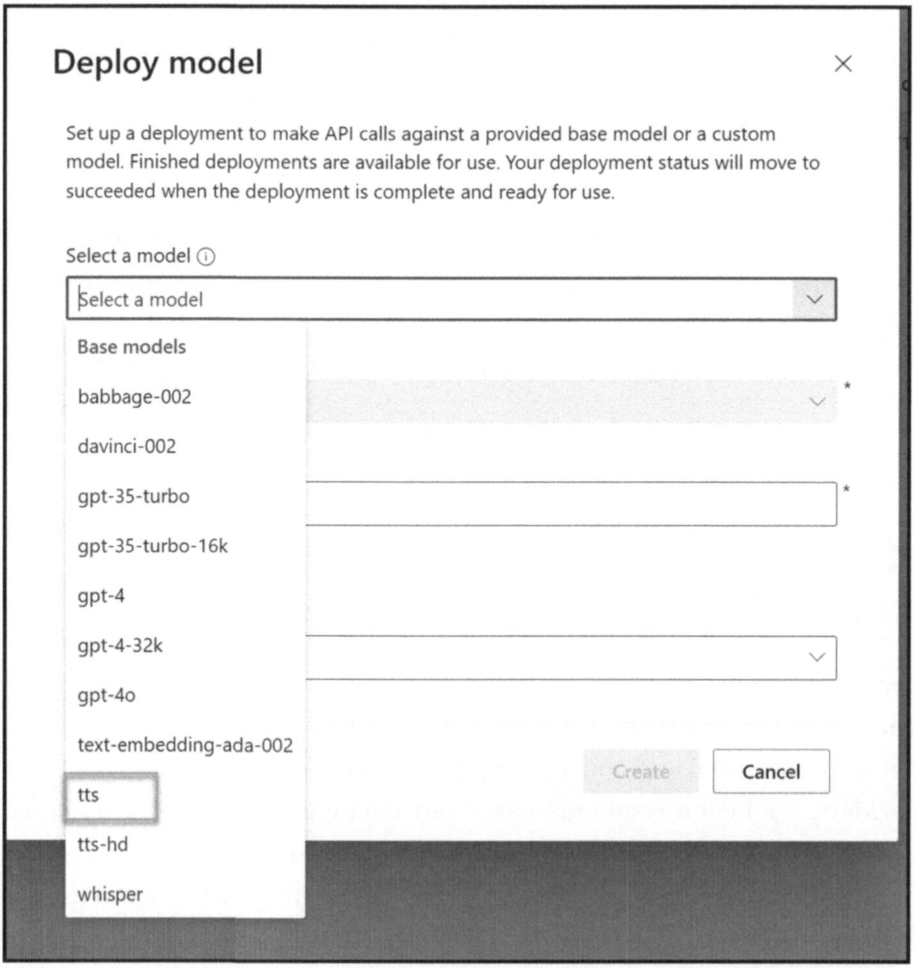

Figure 5-11. *TTS model*

To create an Azure OpenAI resource and deploy a text-to-speech model. Let's start by logging in to Azure using the following Azure CLI command:

```
az login
```

After login, we can run the following lines of code that will do the following:

- Create an Azure Resource Group in the NorthCentralUS region.

- Create an Azure OpenAI resource named aoi-apress-tts-ch55.

- Create an Azure OpenAI deployment for tts.

```
# Create an Azure resource group

az group create --name rg-apress-tts-ch5 --location
northcentralus

# Create an Azure OpenAI resource

az cognitiveservices account create  --name aoi-apress-ai
--location northcentralus --resource-group rg-apress-tts-ch5
--kind OpenAI --sku S0


# Create an Azure OpenAI deployment
az cognitiveservices account deployment create --name aoi-
apress-ai --resource-group rg-apress-tts-ch5 --deployment-name
tts --model-name tts  --model-format OpenAI --model-version "1"
--sku-name "Standard" --sku-capacity "1"
```

After the deployment is completed, verify that the deployment exists in the Azure OpenAI portal (https://oai.azure.com) before proceeding to the next step.

Retrieve Keys

To connect to Azure OpenAI from Postman, copy the Endpoint and API Key from the resource page (Keys and Endpoint).

You can also retrieve the API key using the following Azure CLI commands:

```
az cognitiveservices account keys list --name ACCOUNTNAME
--resource-group RESOURCEGROUPNAME
```

Create Post Request (Postman)

We have everything we need to use the Azure OpenAI text-to-speech service using REST API at this stage.

Open Postman and create a new POST request to use the text-to-speech service using the following details.

Request type	POST
URL	https:// {{ENDPOINTURL}}//openai/deployments/tts/audio/speech?api-version=2024-02-15-preview

Body	{
	"model": "tts-1-hd",
	"input": "Assistants",
	"voice": "nova"
	}

Auth Type	API Key Key = api-key Value = Use API Key from Azure OpenAI Resource Please see Figure 5-6

In this request, we are using the OpenAI voice named Nove. The other available voices are

- Alloy

- Echo

- Fable

- Onyx

- Nova

- Shimmer

To listen to each sound, visit the following OpenAI URL: `https://platform.openai.com/docs/guides/text-to-speech`

Figure 5-12 shows the REST API request.

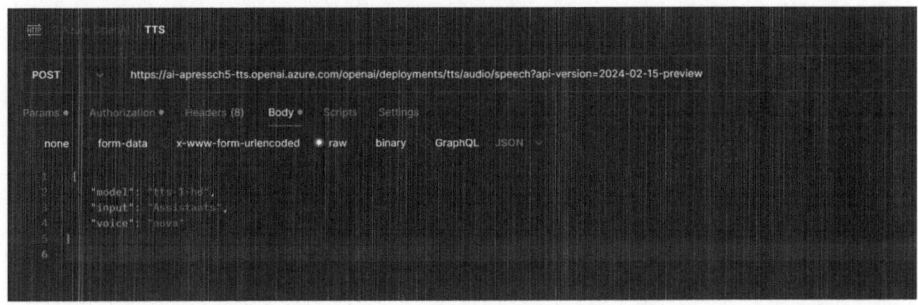

Figure 5-12. *REST API request for Azure text to speech*

The JSON body of the request holds the text that will be converted into speech. In our example, the work Assistants will be converted.

In the request, we are using the 2024-02-15-preview API version. As of writing this book, the following API versions are available:

       2024-02-15-preview

       2024-03-01-preview

       2024-04-01-preview

       2024-05-01-preview

To see the API in action, click the Send button, and you should see an audio player and a play button (Figure 5-13). Click play to play the audio from the text.

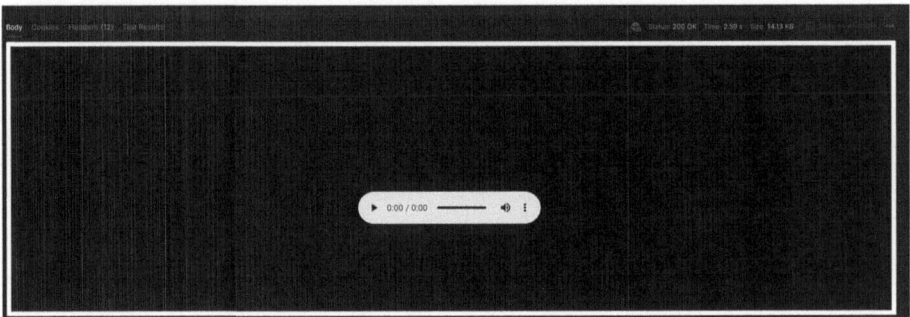

Figure 5-13. *Audio playback*

If you click on the three-dot menu, you will have the option to download the file. In our case, this was just a simple example, but you can add an entire text block and convert it into audio.

Use Azure AI Text-to-Speech Console App

In this section, we are going to create a text-to-speech Console application using C#. This console application will not use the Azure OpenAI API. It will use the Azure AI speech service API.

As of the time of this book, the Azure OpenAI text-to-speech service doesn't have a .NET library.

As we discussed in Chapter 1, Azure AI Services offer a wide range of AI services, and OpenAI is one of them.

The Azure AI Speech service allows us to convert text to speech and speech to text, similar to Azure OpenAI text to speech.

.NET Library

To access the service, we will need to install the following .NET package (also shown in Figure 5-14):

Microsoft.CognitiveServices.Speech

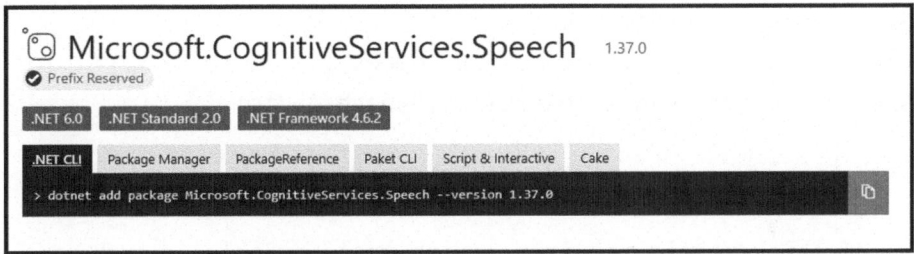

Figure 5-14. *Microsoft Cognitive Services Speech Nuget package*

Create Console Application

To create a Console application using C#, open VS Code.

Open the terminal window in VS Code and create a directory.

```
mkdir Chapter-5
cd Chapter-5
mkdir Texttospeech
dotnet new console
```

Install Package

Install the Speech package by running the following command:

```
dotnet add package Microsoft.CognitiveServices.Speech
--version 1.37.0
```

Program.cs

In the Program.cs file, copy the following code:

```
using System;
using System.IO;
using System.Threading.Tasks;
using Microsoft.CognitiveServices.Speech;
using Microsoft.CognitiveServices.Speech.Audio;

class Program
{
    // This example requires environment variables named
    "SPEECH_KEY" and "SPEECH_REGION"
    static string speechKey = Environment.GetEnvironment
    Variable("SPEECH_KEY");
    static string speechRegion = Environment.GetEnvironment
    Variable("SPEECH_REGION");

    static void OutputSpeechSynthesisResult(SpeechSynthesis
    Result speechSynthesisResult, string text)
    {
        switch (speechSynthesisResult.Reason)
        {
            case ResultReason.SynthesizingAudioCompleted:
                Console.WriteLine($"Speech synthesized for
                text: [{text}]");
                break;
            case ResultReason.Canceled:
                var cancellation = SpeechSynthesisCancellation
                Details.FromResult(speechSynthesisResult);
                Console.WriteLine($"CANCELED: Reason=
                {cancellation.Reason}");
```

```
        if (cancellation.Reason == Cancellation
        Reason.Error)
        {
            Console.WriteLine($"CANCELED: ErrorCode=
            {cancellation.ErrorCode}");
            Console.WriteLine($"CANCELED: ErrorDetails=
            [{cancellation.ErrorDetails}]");
            Console.WriteLine($"CANCELED: Did you
            set the speech resource key and region
            values?");
        }
        break;
    default:
        break;
    }
}

async static Task Main(string[] args)
{
    var speechConfig = SpeechConfig.FromSubscription
    (speechKey, speechRegion);

    // The neural multilingual voice can speak different
    languages based on the input text.
    speechConfig.SpeechSynthesisVoiceName = "en-US-Ava
    MultilingualNeural";

    using (var speechSynthesizer = new SpeechSynthesizer
    (speechConfig))
    {
```

```
        // Get text from the console and synthesize to the
        default speaker.
        Console.WriteLine("Enter some text that you want to
        speak >");
        string text = Console.ReadLine();

        var speechSynthesisResult = await speec
        hSynthesizer.SpeakTextAsync(text);
        OutputSpeechSynthesisResult(speechSynthesisResult,
        text);
    }

    Console.WriteLine("Press any key to exit...");
    Console.ReadKey();
    }
}
```

Create Environment Variables

For the application to connect to the Azure, we need to create the following environment variables.

```
$env:SPEECH_KEY="API KEY"
$env:SPEECH_REGION="Azure SPEECH REGION"
```

For the speech service to work, we need to provide only two variables, speech region location and API Key.

If you are not sure what is your region, you will find it under the Keys and Endpoint section of your speech service (Figure 5-15).

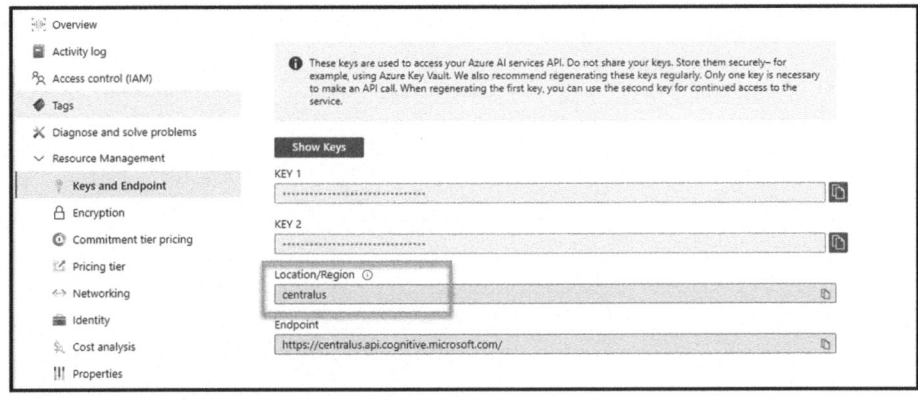

Figure 5-15. *Keys and Endpoint*

Azure AI Studio

In the last section of this chapter, we will cover Azure AI Studio. Azure AI Studio is a one-stop shop AI platform for everything AI.

The platform incorporates many of what is available in the Azure OpenAI portal but also offers the following features:

- Build Copilots

- Chat applications

- Marketplace for AI models from multiple companies (Meta, OpenAI, and more)

- Audit and governance tools

- Build AI websites and applications

Azure AI Studio is available from the following URL `https://ai.azure.com` (Figure 5-16).

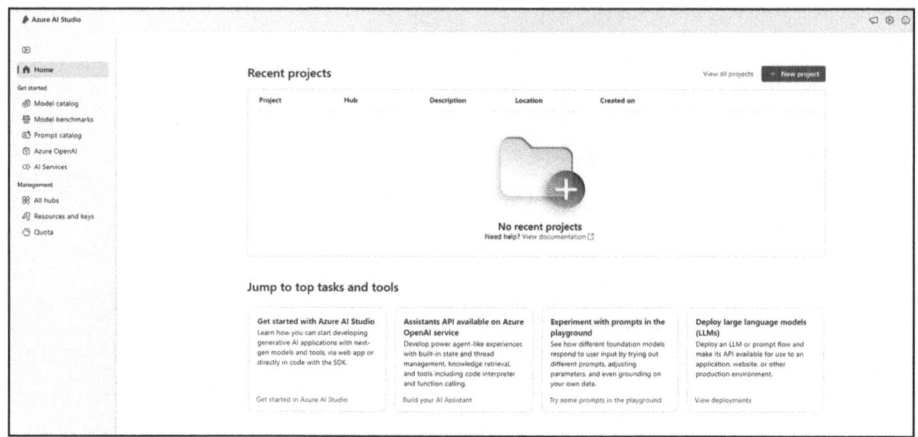

Figure 5-16. *Azure AI Studio home page*

One of the great features of AI Studio is the Model catalog, which offers access to open models from multiple vendors using a single platform and the ability to use the same tools to build AI apps and websites.

If you click on the Model catalog link from the navigation menu, you will see that AI Studio offers 1672 models to choose from and runs a benchmark against them.

Figure 5-17 shows the Model catalog page.

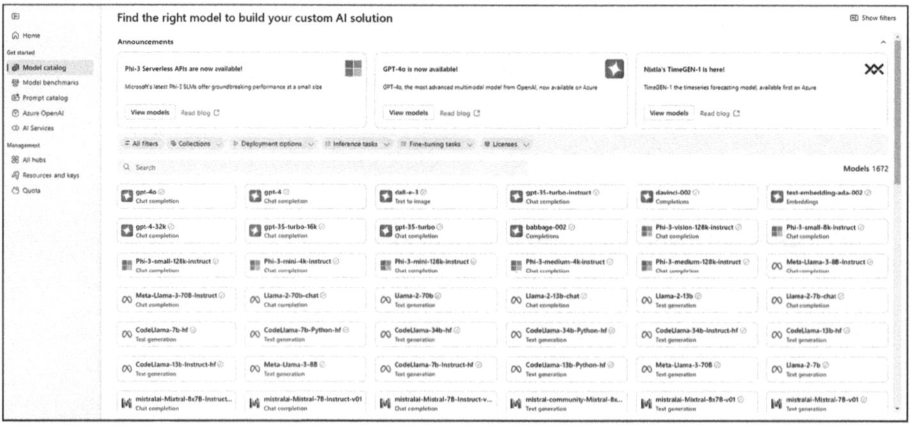

Figure 5-17. *Model catalog*

Create a Chat Playground

To try the capabilities of the AI Portal, I will show you how to create a Chat playground using GPT-4 model.

To get started, from the Azure AI Studio homepage, click New project, as shown in Figure 5-18.

Figure 5-18. *New project*

In AI Studio, a Hub and a Project are top-level logical wrappers that are based on Azure Machine Learning workspaces. As I discussed in Chapter 1, Azure AI is a rebrand of Azure Cognitive and Machine Learning services, and some of the logical structures of Azure AI are based on these services.

When we create a Hub, it provides us with the following:

- Grouping of storage accounts and data

- Project management of resources

- Connectors to Azure Services

- Compute resources for developed solutions.

A project is a direct child resource of a Hub. It provides the following:

- Development tools for building and developing solutions

- Access to data tools like search and more

- Access to storage

- Access to AI models from the catalog

One of the benefits of Hubs is that they provide central governance to AI services under a single logical structure.

When you create a Project (Figure 5-19), you have the option to create a new hub or use an existing one.

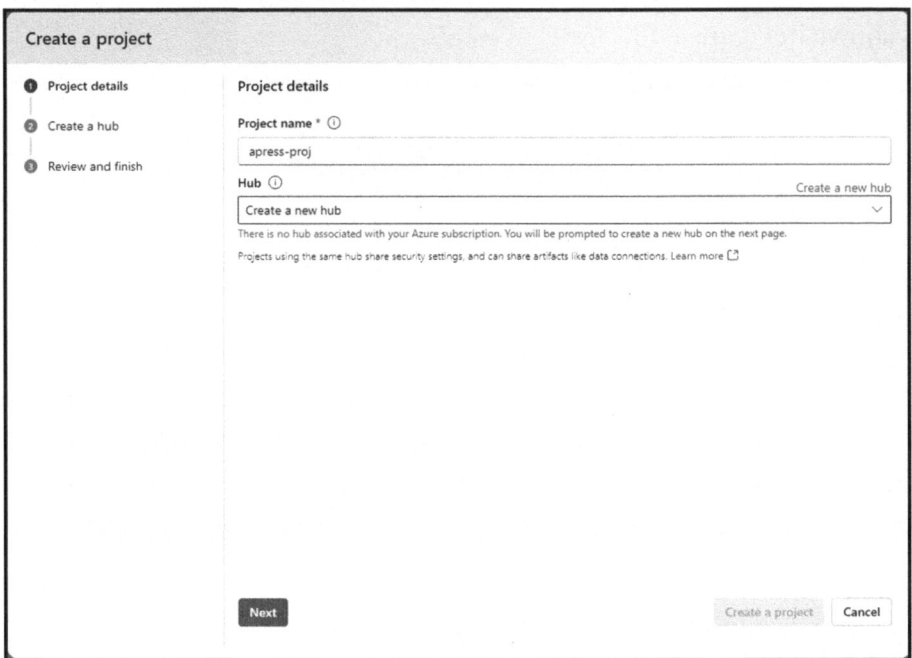

Figure 5-19. *Create a project*

If you click the Create a new hub button, you will have the option to customize your Hub configuration as shown in Figure 5-20.

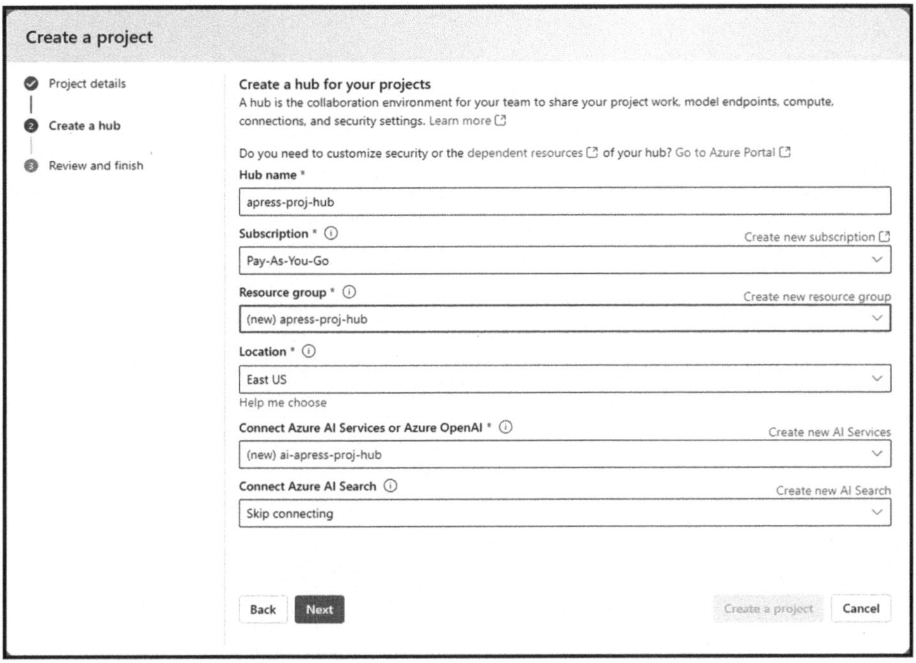

Figure 5-20. *Create a hub*

Note   Please remember to delete Hubs and Projects that are
not in use.

When you create a new Hub, the following services will be provisioned
automatically:

> Resource Group
>
> Storage account
>
> AI Services
>
> Key Vault

Figure 5-21 shows the resources that are created as part of a new Hub.

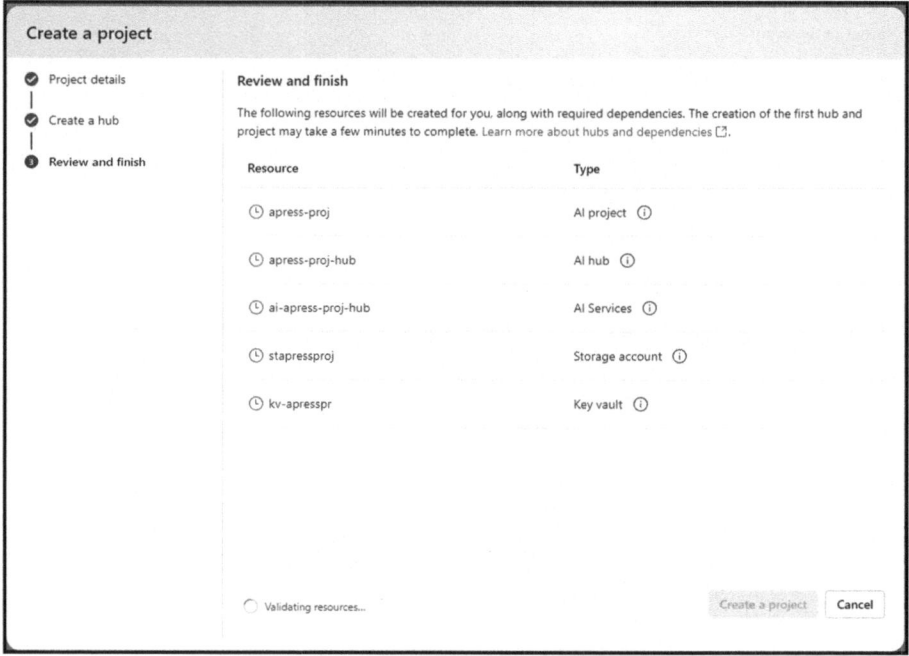

Figure 5-21. *Resources created as part of a new Hub*

From here, the process of creating a Chat playground is like the process of creating a Chat playground in the Azure OpenAI portal. The main difference between the two is that we have the option in the AI Studio to select non-OpenAI models.

Deploy a Model

To deploy a model, click the Deployment button in the left navigation menu (Figure 5-22).

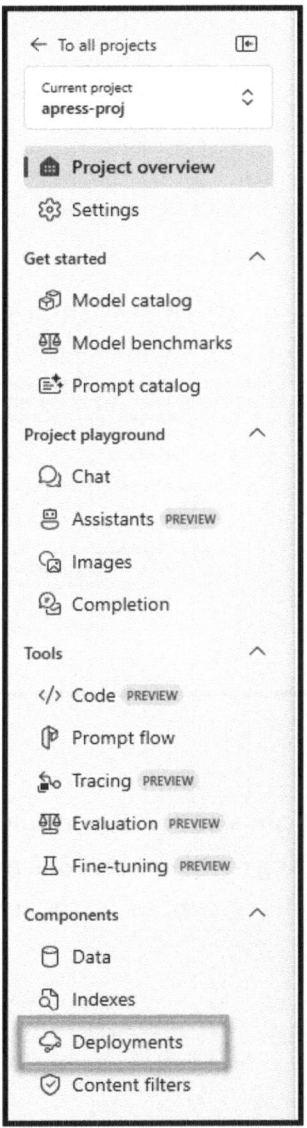

Figure 5-22. *Deployments*

Click new deployment, and from the select a model page, select gpt-4 as shown in Figure 5-23.

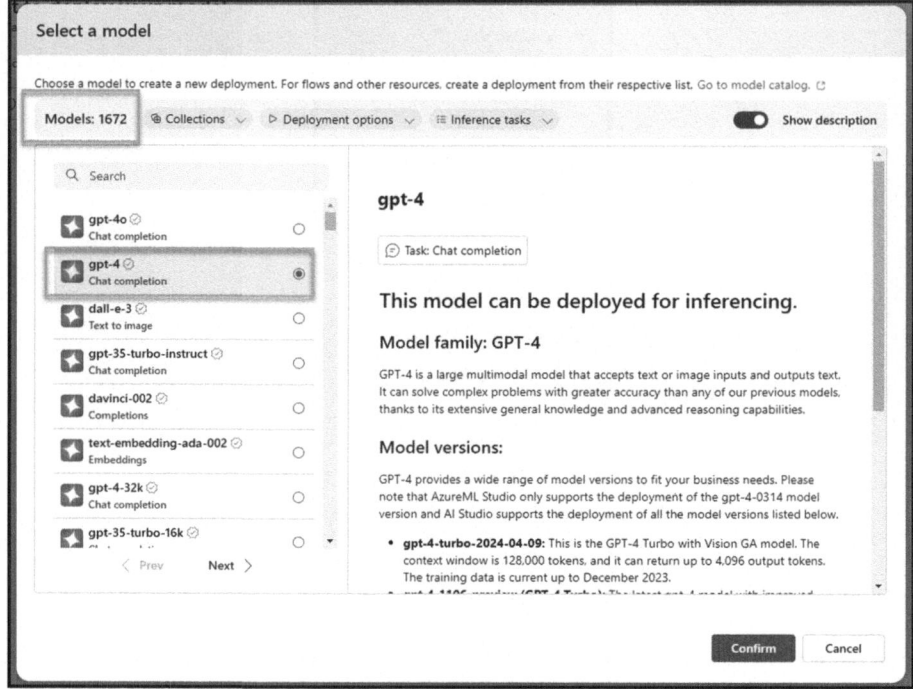

Figure 5-23. *Select a model*

From Figure 5-23, you can also see the number of models available for deployment. As of the writing of this book, 1672 models are available.

From the deploy a model screen, select the model version and set the deployment name (Figure 5-24).

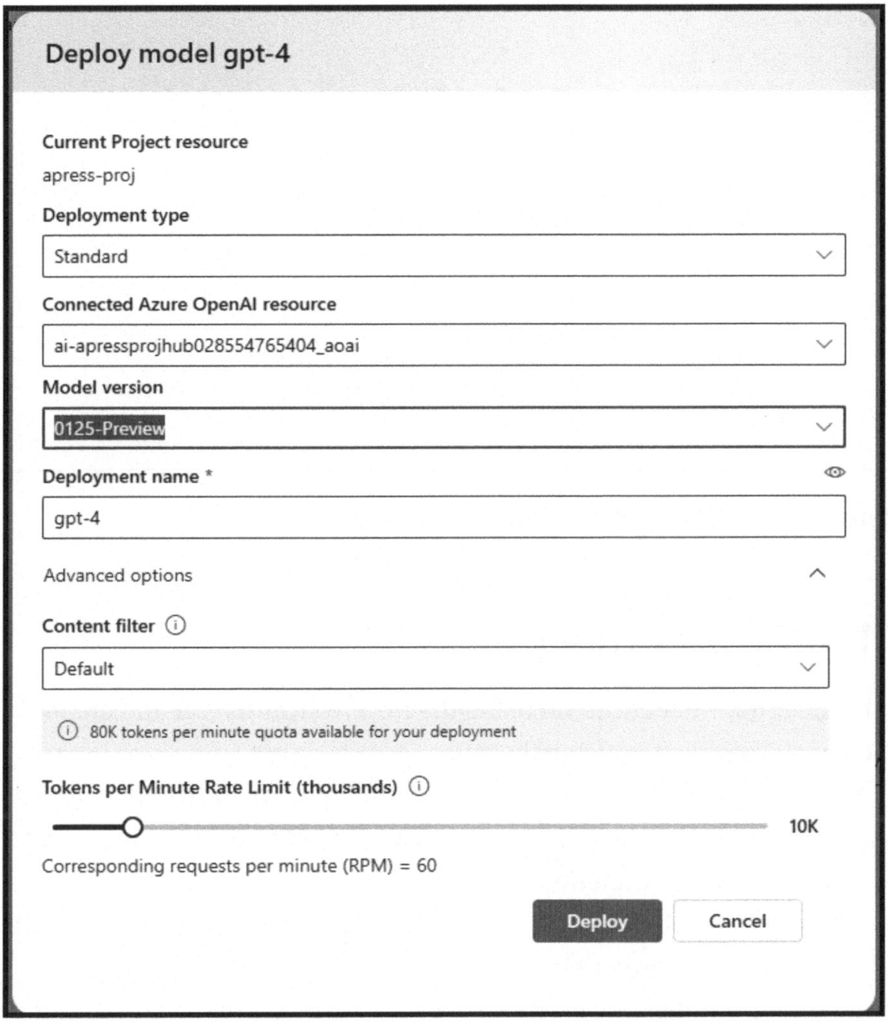

Deploy model gpt-4

Current Project resource
apress-proj

Deployment type

| Standard | ∨ |

Connected Azure OpenAI resource

| ai-apressprojhub028554765404_aoai | ∨ |

Model version

| 0125-Preview | ∨ |

Deployment name *   👁

| gpt-4 |

Advanced options   ∧

Content filter ⓘ

| Default | ∨ |

ⓘ 80K tokens per minute quota available for your deployment

Tokens per Minute Rate Limit (thousands) ⓘ

○─── 10K

Corresponding requests per minute (RPM) = 60

Deploy   Cancel

Figure 5-24. *Deploy model*

Once the model is deployed, click the Chat button from the navigation menu on the left side.

In the Chat Playground window (Figure 5-25), select the newly deployed model and follow the steps discussed in Chapter 3.

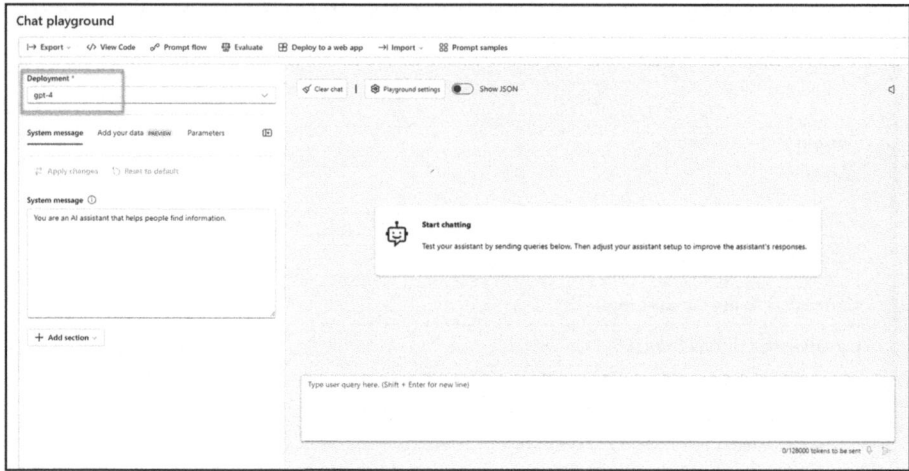

Figure 5-25.   *Chat playground*

Chapter Summary

In this chapter, we focused on using the new Assistants API and created a C# Console application using the API.

We also learned how to use the API with Postman and create an Assistant. We also discussed how the Assistants API is more advanced compared to Chat completions.

When you use the new API, make sure you understand the Assistants API object and components.

In addition to API, we learned how to use the Azure OpenAI Text to speech API and also the Azure AI Speech service.

Make sure you understand the difference between the two services.

In the last section of the book, we covered the new Azure AI Studio and the capabilities the new portal offers.

CHAPTER 6

GPT-4o, DALL-E, and Whisper

In this chapter, we will learn how to use the new GPT-4o AI model, how to generate images with DALL-E, convert speech to text with Whisper, and use speech-to-speech chat with GPT4.

GPT-4o

In May 2024, OpenAI released its flagship AI model, GPT-4o. The model is available in Azure OpenAI and provides groundbreaking capabilities.

The model's name, o, refers to the word Omni, which means multimodal and integrates the following capabilities:

- Test

- Vision

- Audio

It offers a response time of 232 milliseconds for audio inputs, similar to a human response time during a conversation. It also generates text 50% faster and cost 50% less.

GPT-4o provides the most advanced AI capabilities by accepting input combinations in text and audio.

GPT-4o is considered groundbreaking because it opens the door for developers to write applications that can interact with people naturally using all forms of communication (vision, voice, and text).

The model is available only in two US Azure regions and is accessible from the Azure OpenAI playground, REST and SDK.

Another interesting point about the GPT-4o is that it is also the most affordable flagship model compared to the GPT-4 Turbo. This change is a sign of the economy of scale of AI infrastructure.

Deploying GPT-4o

The following table shows the model versions and details.

Model Name	Context Windows	Training Data
gpt-4o	128,000 tokens	Up to October 2023
gpt-4o-2024-05-13	128,000 tokens	Up to October 2023

To access the model, we need to deploy an Azure OpenAI resource in the following regions.

Region	Deployment Type
Sweden Central	Standard
Korea Central	Provisioned
Sweden Central	Provisioned
Switzerland North	Provisioned
West US 3	Provisioned

To deploy a GPT4-o model, we need to use the following details in the deployment.

Model Name	Version
Gpt-4o	2024-05-13

Deploy a GPT4-o Model Using Azure CLI

To get started with GPT4-o, we need to deploy an Azure OpenAI resource in a supported region first. Once deployed, we will deploy GPT-4o model.

For this task, I will use the following Azure CLI. Before you run the code, make sure you login to Azure first using the following command:

```
Az login
```

Run the code to deploy GPT-4o.

```
# Define variables
resourceGroupName="rg-apress-ch6"
location="SwedenCentral"
accountName="aoi-apress-ai"
kind="OpenAI"
sku="S0"
deploymentName="gpt-4"
modelName="gpt-4o"
modelFormat="OpenAI"
modelVersion="2024-05-13"
skuName="Standard"
skuCapacity="1"

# Create an Azure resource group
az group create --name $resourceGroupName --location $location
```

```
# Create an Azure OpenAI resource
az cognitiveservices account create --name $accountName
--location $location --resource-group $resourceGroupName --kind
$kind --sku $sku

# Create an Azure OpenAI deployment
az cognitiveservices account deployment create --name
$accountName --resource-group $resourceGroupName --deployment-
name $deploymentName --model-name $modelName --model-format
$modelFormat --model-version $modelVersion --sku-name $skuName
--sku-capacity $skuCapacity
```

Check Deployment

Once the deployment is completed, open the Azure OpenAI portal
(https://oai.azure.com).

Select your deployment and confirm that the deployed model version
is 2024-05-13 and the model name is gpt-4o.

Figure 6-1 shows deployment details.

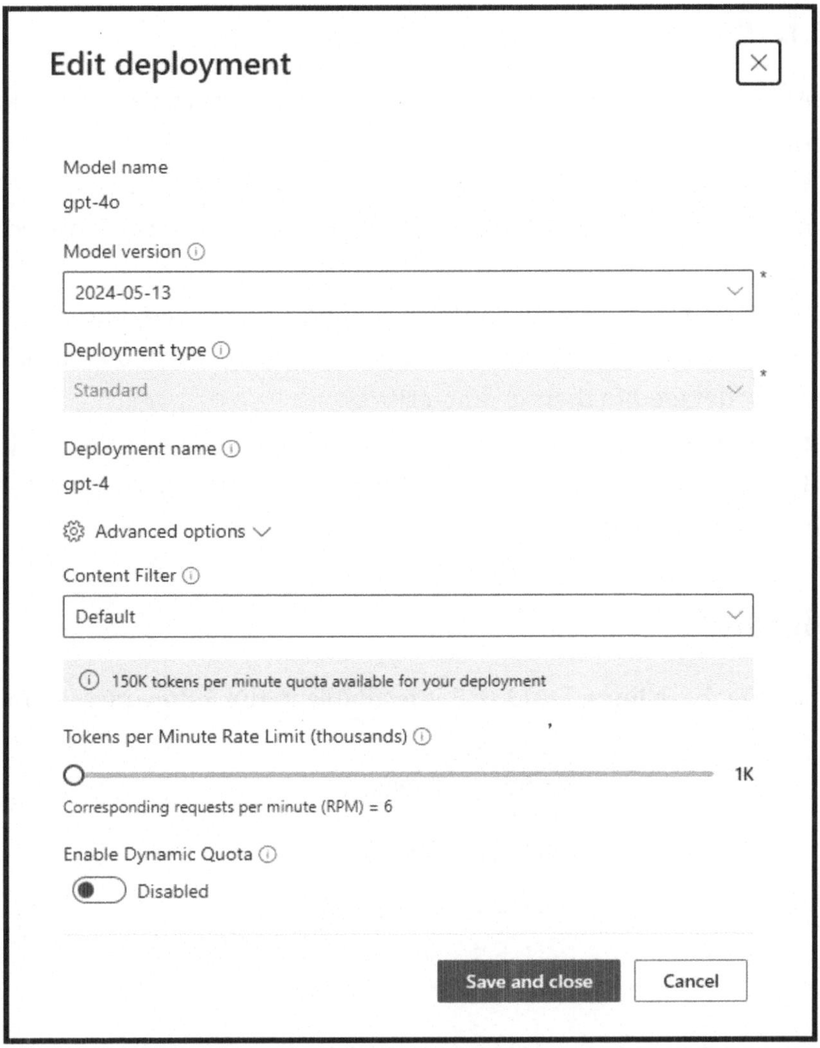

Figure 6-1. *Deployment details*

At this stage, our GPT-4o model is deployed and ready to use. To use it, we can use the code base we used in the previous chapters.

DALL-E

OpenAI DALL-E is an AI model that creates images and artwork that look real from a text input.

The first DALL-E model was introduced in early 2021. In early 2022, OpenAI released the current model, DALL-E 2, which offers advanced capabilities.

The latest DALL-E model, DALL-E 3, offers the most advanced capabilities and a better understanding of text input, which means images can be very detailed in their characteristics.

Azure OpenAI services also offer the DALL-E and allow us to use the same tools we have used so far in this book to generate high-resolution images from text prompts.

Availability

As of writing these lines, DALL-E 3 is available in the following regions.

Model	Region
DALL-E 3	EastUS
DALL-E 3	AustraliaEast
DALL-E 3	SwedenCentral

So, if you decide to use DALL-E, make sure you have an Azure OpenAI resource in one of the above regions.

The process to access a DALL-E model is the same as accessing a GPT-4 and GPT-4o. First, we must create an Azure OpenAI resource in a region where the model is available. After deploying a resource, we need to create a deployment with a DALL-E 3 model, as you will see shortly.

Create a Deployment and Model

To get started with DALL-E, we need to create an Azure OpenAI resource and deployment. Since DALL-E is available in the same region as the GPT-4o we deployed in the previous section, we can use the same resource but change the model deployment.

The complete code is shown as follows with changes to the following variables: deploymentName, modelName and modelVersion

Azure CLI: Deployment Code

```
# Define variables
resourceGroupName="rg-apress-ch6"
location="SwedenCentral"
accountName="aoi-apress-ai"
kind="OpenAI"
sku="S0"
deploymentName="dall-e-3"
modelName="dall-e-3"
modelFormat="OpenAI"
modelVersion="3.0"
skuName="Standard"
skuCapacity="1"

# Create an Azure resource group
az group create --name $resourceGroupName --location $location

# Create an Azure OpenAI resource
az cognitiveservices account create --name $accountName
--location $location --resource-group $resourceGroupName --kind
$kind --sku $sku

# Create an Azure OpenAI deployment
```

```
az cognitiveservices account deployment create --name
$accountName --resource-group $resourceGroupName --deployment-
name $deploymentName --model-name $modelName --model-format
$modelFormat --model-version $modelVersion --sku-name $skuName
--sku-capacity $skuCapacity
```

After deploying the code, open the Azure OpenAI portal, and verify that the DALL-E deployment was created successfully, as shown in Figure 6-2.

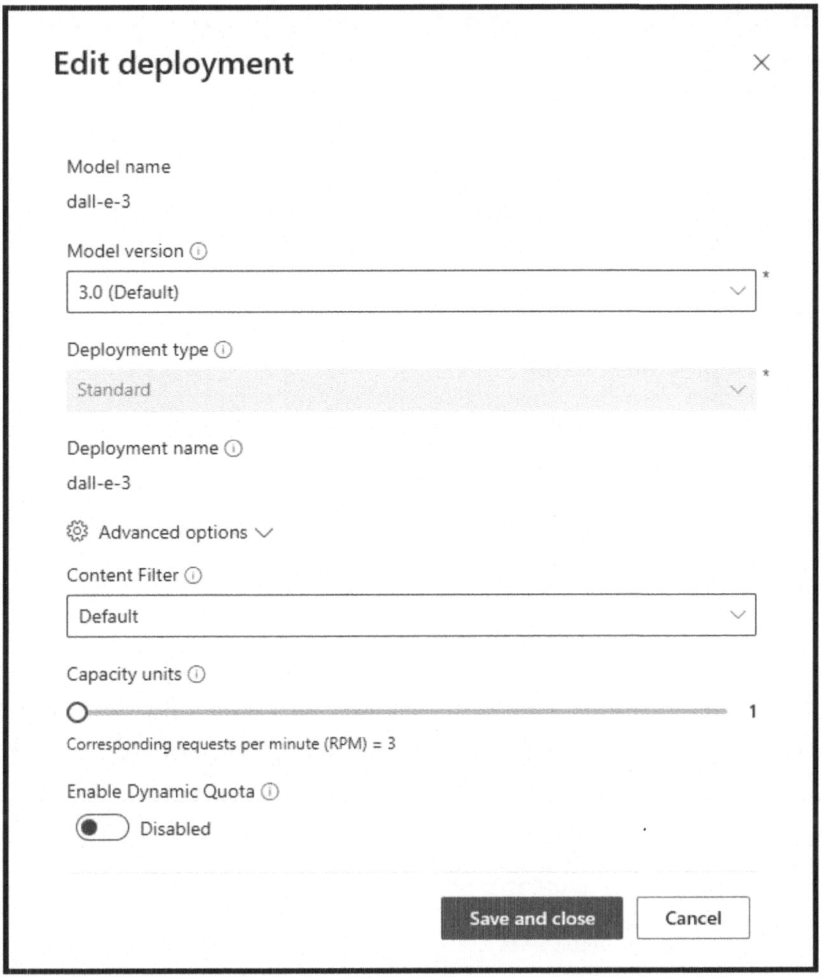

Figure 6-2. *DALL-E deployment*

Now that we have the deployment part out of the way, let's create a REST API request to generate an image using the Postman API client.

Generate Images with Azure OpenAI Service and Postman

To generate an image from a text prompt using the DALL-E REST API protocol, we need the following details:

- Azure OpenAI resource endpoint URL

- API Key from the Azure OpenAI resource

- Deployment name

To retrieve the first two items, open the Azure OpenAI resource we deployed in the previous section (Figure 6-3).

Click Keys and Endpoint and copy the following two items:

- Key 1

- Endpoint

The last item that we need is the deployment name. If you used the Azure CLI deployment code, the name of the deployment is `dall-e-3`.

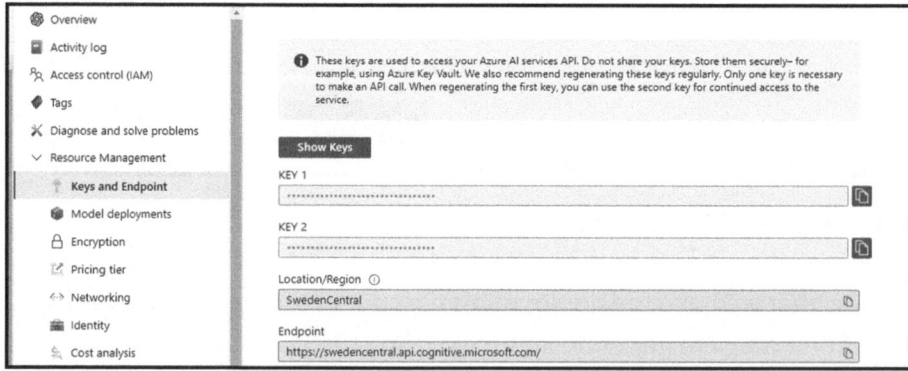

Figure 6-3. *Keys and Endpoint*

Create POST Request and Generate Image

Now that we have all the necessary details, open Postman and create a post request with the following details.

Request Type	POST
URL	https{{ENDPOINT URL}}/openai/deployments/{{DEPLOYMENT NAME}}/images/generations?api-version=2024-05-01-preview

Body	{
	    "prompt":"Please Create a cover image for a book called Getting Started with Azure OpenAI",
	    "n": 1,
	    "size": "1024x1024",
	    "quality": "hd",
	    "response_format": "url",
	    "style": "vivid"
	}

Authorization	Api-key – {{API KEY}}
Params	Api-version=2024-05-01-preview

Figure 6-4 shows what the request looks like in Postman.

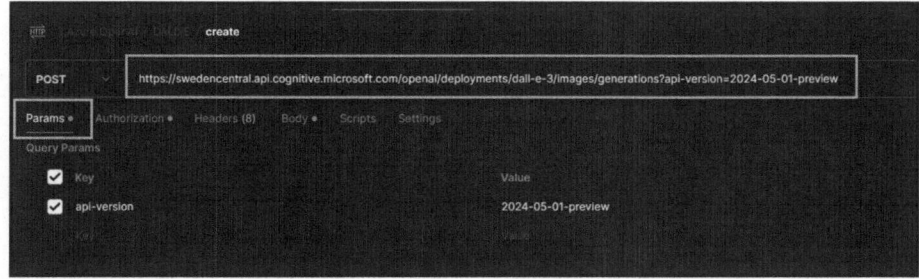

Figure 6-4. *POST request*

The Body of the request is shown in Figure 6-5.

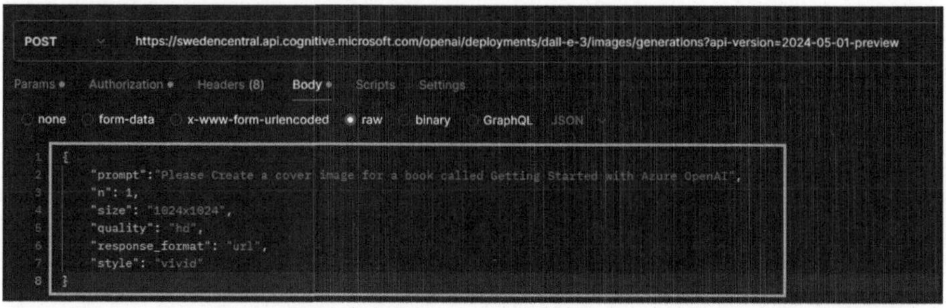

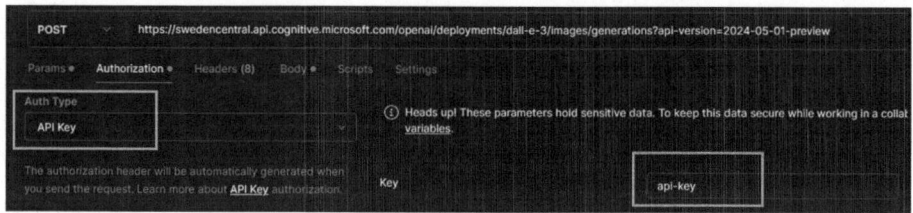

Figure 6-5. *Body of the request*

The Authorization tab is shown in Figure 6-6. Add your API key in the Value area and use Header.

Figure 6-6. *Authorization tab*

Customize Request Body

In our example, I have customized the request body; however, you can further customize it with the following options that are available. Simply change the request body with the available options.

Parameter	Type	Required?	Default	Description
prompt	string	Yes		Images or image description 4000 max characters
n	integer	No	1	The number of images to generate. DALL-E 3, supports 1 image
size	string	No	1024x1024	Generated image size (options): 1792x1024 1024x1024 1024x1792
quality	string	No	standard	Image quality (options): hd standard
response_ format	string	No	url	Generated image returned format: url b64_json
style	string	No	vivid	Generated image style (options): Natural vivid (realistic/dramatic)

Send a Request and Download the Image

To review the results, send the request. The result will return in the form of a URL. Copy the returned URL to your browser.

The returned prompt and URL is shown as follows:

```
"revised_prompt": "Design a cover for a book titled
'Getting Started with Azure OpenAI'. The cover
features a letter 'A' that's stylized to represent a
futuristic AI design. It is set against the backdrop
of a night sky filled with stars, symbolizing the vast
```

229

```
potential of AI. The 'Azure' colour theme dominates
the cover, with different shades of blue blending
harmoniously. The title of the book is neatly centered
towards the top, with large, bold letters standing out
against the backdrop. The overall design communicates
a sense of cutting-edge technology and boundless
possibilities.",
    "url": "RETURNED URL"
```

In Figure 6-7, you can see the generated image.

Note   Images are deleted after 60 minutes.

Figure 6-7. *Generated image*

Note   When using the DALL-E API, make sure that you use the latest API version.

Create a C# Console App with DALL-E

We can also use the Azure SDK for .NET to create a console application that generates images using the Azure OpenAI DALL-E model.

In this section, we will create a console application that generates images. We can use our existing deployment for this purpose.

Set Environment Variables

Before continuing, make sure you set the following environment variables:

- Azure OpenAI Whisper endpoint

- API Key

To set the following environment variables using PowerShell, run the following commands from VS Code terminal window:

```
$env:AZURE_OPENAI_ENDPOINT="ENDPOINT URL"
$env:AZURE_OPENAI_API_KEY="API KEY"
```

For this deployment, note the name of the DALL-E model; if you followed the deployment code, it should be dall-e-3.

Create Console App

From your VS Code terminal window, create a directory using the following command:

```
mkdir DALL-E
```

After creating the directory, create a console application

```
dotnet new console
```

Install the Azure OpenAI library

```
dotnet add package Azure.AI.OpenAI --version 1.0.0-beta.17
```

Copy the following code to Program.cs:

```
using static System.Environment;
using System.IO;
using System.Threading.Tasks;
using Azure.AI.OpenAI;
```

```csharp
namespace Azure.AI.OpenAI.Tests.Samples
{
    public partial class GenerateImages
    {
        // Get the environment variable
        public static async Task Main(string[] args)
        {
            string endpoint = GetEnvironmentVariable
            ("AZURE_OPENAI_ENDPOINT");
            string key = GetEnvironmentVariable("AZURE_OPENAI_
            API_KEY");

            OpenAIClient client = new(new Uri(endpoint),
            new AzureKeyCredential(key));

            // Get the image generations asynchronously
            Response<ImageGenerations> imageGenerations = await
            client.GetImageGenerationsAsync(
                new ImageGenerationOptions()
                {
                    DeploymentName = "dall-e-3",
                    Prompt = "Create a book cover for a book
                    called Getting Started with Azure",
                    Size = ImageSize.Size1024x1024,

                });

            // Get the image URI from the response:
            Uri imageUri = imageGenerations.Value.Data[0].Url;

            // Print the image URI
            Console.WriteLine(imageUri);
        }
    }
}
```

Save the file and run it using the following command:

```
dotnet run
```

The program should return the URL that contains the URL for the generated image.

DALL-E Playground

If you prefer to test using a GUI interface, you can use the Azure OpenAI Studio DALL-E Playground, available on the Azure OpenAI Studio portal.

From the portal, click the DALL-Playground as shown in Figure 6-8.

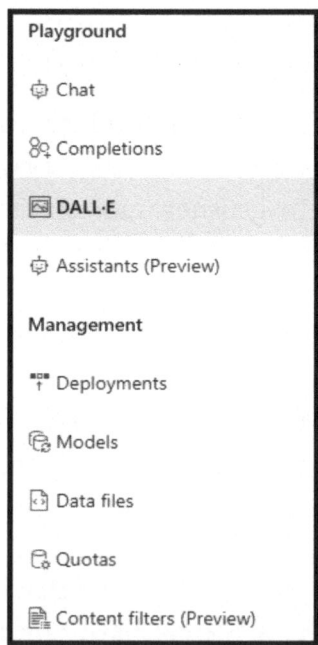

Figure 6-8. *DALL-E*

Select the DALL-E deployment from the DALL-E playground page, and use the search bar to generate images from text.

As shown in Figure 6-9, I used the prompt search to describe the image I would like to generate.

Figure 6-9. *DALL-E Playground*

Whisper

The Microsoft Azure OpenAI Whisper model allows us to convert speech to text (also known as transcribing audio). The model is configured to accept audio files and convert them into text.

The following table outlines the capabilities of the Whisper model. It is important to note that the Whisper model is incapable of real-time transcription.

Capability	Output
Transcription of prerecording audio files	Captions and subtitles
Transcript phone calls recording	Call summary and sentiment
Transcript of meeting recording	Meeting summary and action item
Voice agent	Call routing and voice response
Translate audio from another language into English	Translation

Azure AI Services also offers an audio-to-text service via the Azure AI Speech service. The main benefits of using the Azure AI Speech service are

- Real-time transcription
- Transcription of large files (25MB and above with a limit of 1GB)
- Use batch file

The Azure OpenAI Whisper service has the following benefits:

- Quick transcription of audio files
- Add a prompt with instructions to the model
- Support multiple file format (MP3, MP4, mpweg, mpga m4a, wav and wbm)

Whisper is currently available in the following Azure regions:

- East United States 2

- North Central United States

- Norway East

- South India

- Sweden Central

- West Europe

Create a Deployment and Model

To deploy the Azure OpenAI model, we will use a similar Azure CLI deployment and will use the Sweden Central region.

The model details are as follows.

Model Name	Version
whisper	001

Azure CLI: Deployment Code

The following Azure CLI code will deploy an Azure OpenAI resource with the Whisper model:

```
# Define variables
resourceGroupName="rg-apress-ch6"
location="SwedenCentral"
accountName="aoi-apress-ai"
kind="OpenAI"
sku="S0"
```

```
deploymentName="whisper"
modelName="whisper"
modelFormat="OpenAI"
modelVersion="001"
skuName="Standard"
skuCapacity="1"

# Create an Azure resource group
az group create --name $resourceGroupName --location $location

# Create an Azure OpenAI resource
az cognitiveservices account create --name $accountName
--location $location --resource-group $resourceGroupName --kind
$kind --sku $sku

# Create an Azure OpenAI deployment
az cognitiveservices account deployment create --name
$accountName --resource-group $resourceGroupName --deployment-
name $deploymentName --model-name $modelName --model-format
$modelFormat --model-version $modelVersion --sku-name $skuName
--sku-capacity $skuCapacity
```

Once you deploy the services, open the Azure OpenAI portal and verify the model was deployed successfully (Figure 6-10).

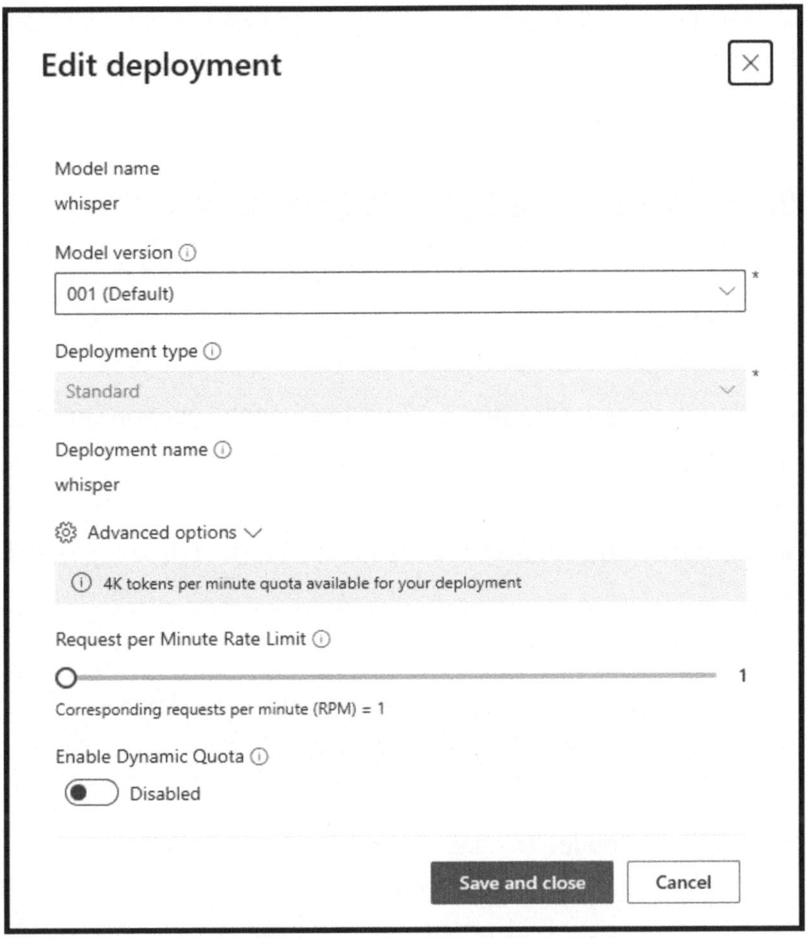

Figure 6-10. *Whisper deployment*

Convert Speech to Text

In this exercise, we are going past the Whisper deployment and model an MP3 file that contains audio.

The audio in this exercise is generated using Azure AI Speech service and the text-to-speech exercise we completed in Chapter 5.

First, I will generate an audio file using Postman and Azure AI Speech. Once I have the audio file, I will send it to Whisper using a PowerShell call using a REST API Post request.

Generate Audio Using Text to Speech

Let's start with generating an audio file using Postman and the Azure AI Speech service.

Note   Please review Chapter 5, "Text to Speech" section, for details step-by-step.

Open Postman and create a Post request with the following details.

Request Type	**POST**
URL	{{ENDPOINT URL/openai/deployments/tts/audio/speech? api-version=2024-02-15-preview

Body	{
	    "model": "tts-1-hd",
	    "input": "If you prefer to test using a GUI interface, you can use the Azure OpenAI Studio DALL-E Playground, available on the Azure OpenAI Studio portal."
	    ,
	    "voice": "nova"
	}

Authorization	Api-key — {{API KEY}}
Params	Api-version=2024-02-15-preview

The post request URL and Parameters are shown in Figure 6-11. Make sure you use the endpoint URL that belongs to your Azure AI Speech service.

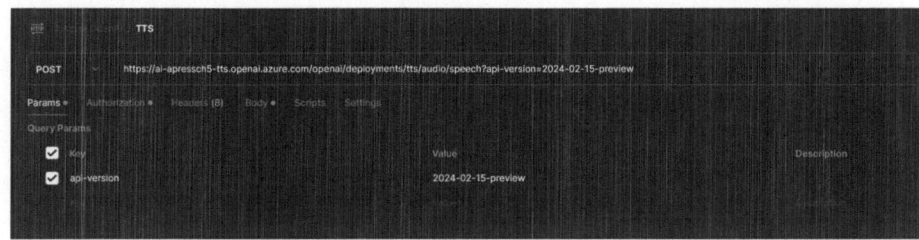

Figure 6-11. *Post request*

To pass the service, we need to include the text we would like to convert to audio in the body of the request.

The body of the request should look like this:

```
{
    "model": "tts-1-hd",
    "input": "If you prefer to test using a GUI interface,
    you can use the Azure OpenAI Studio DALL-E Playground,
    available on the Azure OpenAI Studio portal."
    ,
    "voice": "nova"
}
```

Figure 6-12 shows the request body in Postman.

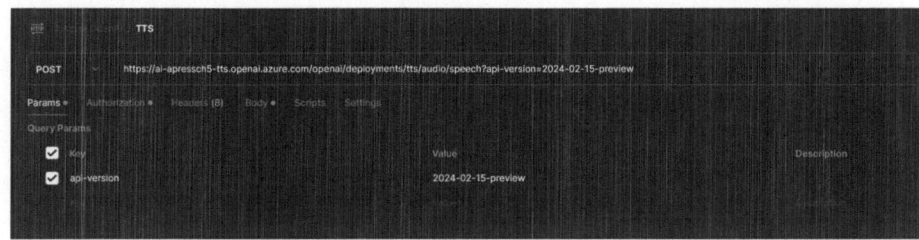

Figure 6-12. *TTS request body*

After you send the request, the audio file will be ready to download from the Postman menu.

From the audio file, click More options (Figure 6-13).

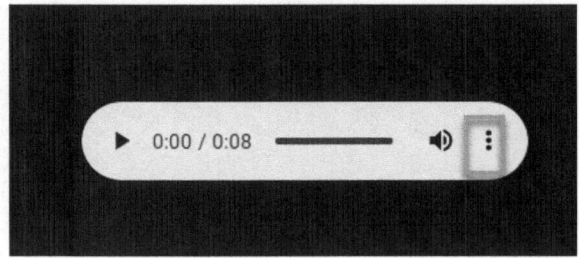

Figure 6-13. *Audio file controller*

Click Download to download the file (Figure 6-14).

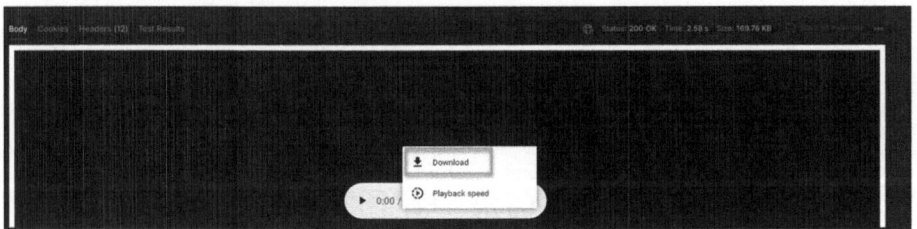

Figure 6-14. *Download*

Now we have an audio file we can send Whisper for transcription.

Set Environment Variables

Before continuing, make sure you set the following environment variables:

- Azure OpenAI Whisper endpoint
- API Key

To set the following environment variables using PowerShell, run the following commands from VS Code terminal window:

```
$env:AZURE_OPENAI_ENDPOINT="ENDPOINT URL"
$env:AZURE_OPENAI_API_KEY="API KEY"
```

PowerShell REST

We will use the following PowerShell script to send the audio file to Whisper. Ensure you copy the audio file in the same script directory.

```
# Azure OpenAI variables
$openai = @{
    api_key     = $Env:AZURE_OPENAI_API_KEY
    api_base    = $Env:AZURE_OPENAI_ENDPOINT
    api_version = '2024-02-01'  # API version
    name        = 'whisper'     # Deployment name
}

# Header for authentication
$headers = [ordered]@{
    'api-key' = $openai.api_key
}

# Audio file to transcribe
$form = @{ file = get-item -path './download.mp3' }

# REST API URL
$url = "$($openai.api_base)/openai/deployments/$($openai.name)
/audio/transcriptions?api-version=$($openai.api_version)"

$response = Invoke-RestMethod -Uri $url -Headers $headers -Form
$form -Method Post -ContentType 'multipart/form-data'
return $response.text # Return the transcribed text
```

Save the script and run it from the terminal window using the following:

```
.\Whisper_PoweShell.ps1
```

The transcription should be:

If you prefer to test using a GUI interface, you can use the Azure OpenAI Studio DALL-E Playground, available on the Azure OpenAI Studio portal.

GPT-4 Turbo with Vision

https://learn.microsoft.com/en-us/azure/ai-services/openai/gpt-v-quickstart?tabs=image%2Ccommand-line&pivots=rest-api

In the last section of this book, we are going to use GPT-4 Turbo with Vision. GPT-4 Vision allows us to input an image and ask the model to describe it.

Since we have used DALL-E to generate images from text, we are going to ask the Vision model to describe the generated image.

For this exercise, we will create a Vision deployment using Azure CLI and ask it to describe an image using the Chat playground interface.

Create a Deployment and Model

To create a GPT-4 Turbo with Vision resource and deployment, we need to use the following Azure CLI code:

```
# Define variables
resourceGroupName="rg-apress-ch6"
location="SwedenCentral"
accountName="aoi-apress-ai"
kind="OpenAI"
sku="S0"
```

```
deploymentName="vision"
modelName="gpt-4"
modelFormat="OpenAI"
modelVersion="vision-preview"
skuName="Standard"
skuCapacity="1"

# Create an Azure resource group
az group create --name $resourceGroupName --location $location

# Create an Azure OpenAI resource
az cognitiveservices account create --name $accountName
--location $location --resource-group $resourceGroupName --kind
$kind --sku $sku

# Create an Azure OpenAI deployment
az cognitiveservices account deployment create --name
$accountName --resource-group $resourceGroupName --deployment-
name $deploymentName --model-name $modelName --model-format
$modelFormat --model-version $modelVersion --sku-name $skuName
--sku-capacity $skuCapacity
```

To verify the deployment, open the Azure OpenAI deployment and make sure it looks like Figure 6-15.

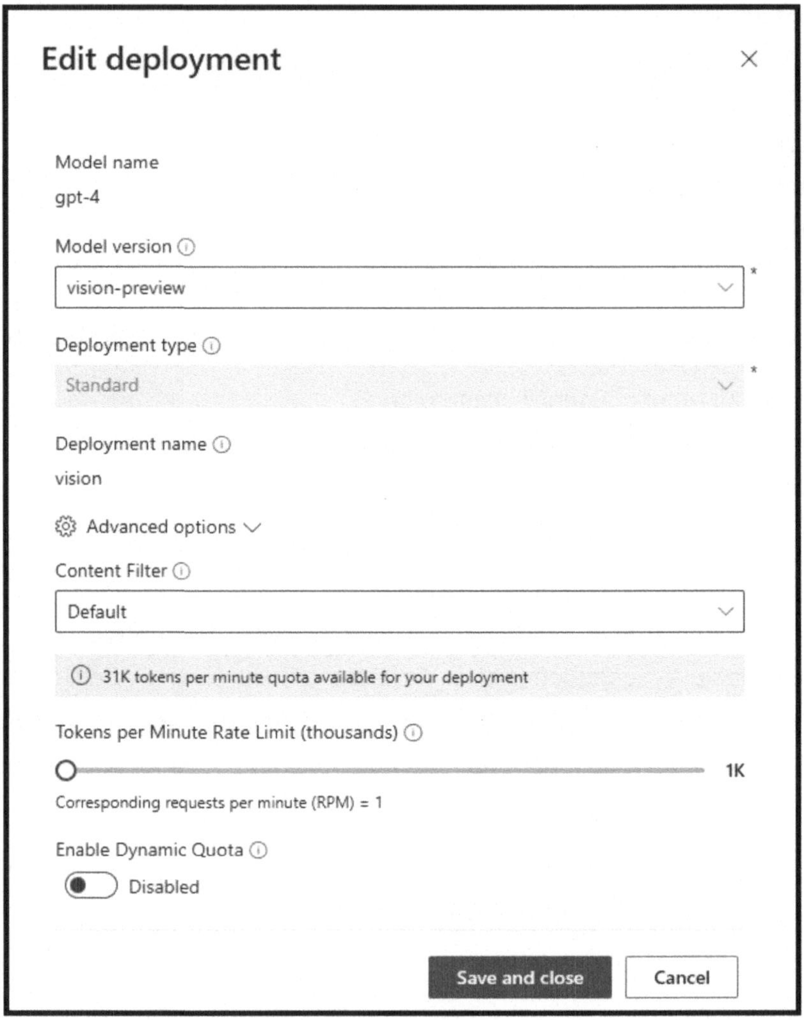

Figure 6-15. *Vision preview*

Use GPT-4 Vision on Images

To test the Vision model, Click the Chat link from the Azure OpenAI Studio (Figure 6-16).

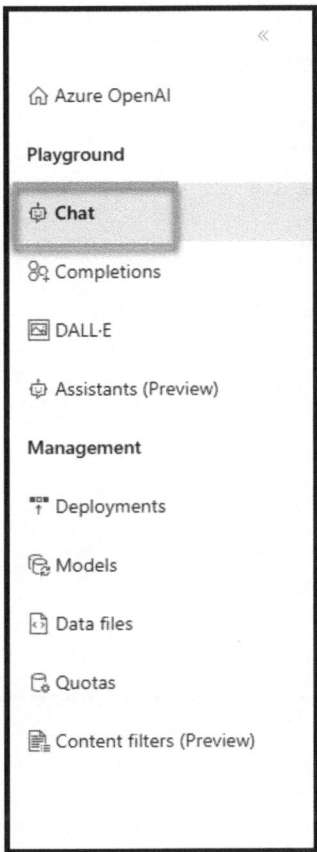

Figure 6-16. *Chat playground*

From the Chat playground, make sure the deployment is set to vision (Figure 6-17).

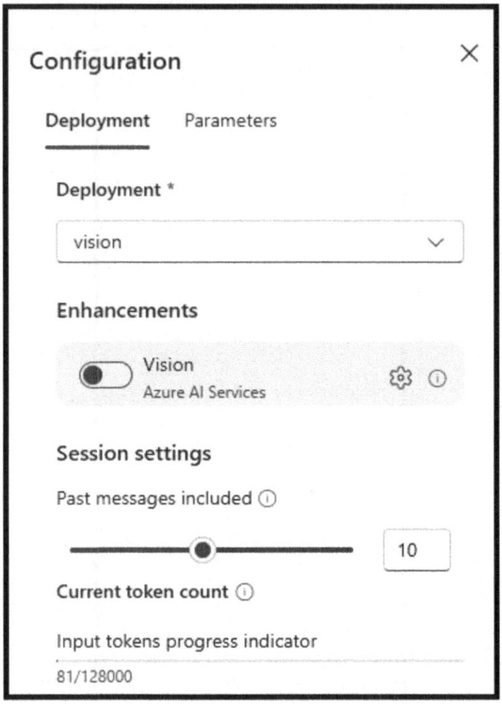

Configuration   ×

Deployment   Parameters

Deployment *

vision   ⌄

Enhancements

Vision
Azure AI Services   {🔧} ⓘ

Session settings

Past messages included ⓘ

──────────●──────────   10

Current token count ⓘ

Input tokens progress indicator
81/128000

Figure 6-17. *Vision*

To upload an image, use the attach button located on the chat windows
(Figure 6-18).

Figure 6-18. *Attach*

In the chat window, ask the model a question about the image. In my case, I will ask it what do you see (Figure 6-19).

Figure 6-19. *Ask the vision model a question about an image*

You can see the model's answer in Figure 6-20.

I see an image of a book with a stylized cover design. The book's title is "Getting Started with Azure OpenAI," which suggests it is about how to begin working with OpenAI technologies on Microsoft's Azure cloud platform. The cover features a large letter "A" in the center with a circuit-like design and glowing neon-blue accents, creating a futuristic tech feel. The background consists of a night sky with stars and clouds, and a grid on the bottom that resembles a digital landscape or a reference to virtual reality. The overall aesthetic of the cover is sleek and modern, likely intended to appeal to those interested in technology and artificial intelligence.

Figure 6-20. *Model's reply*

Chapter Summary

In this last chapter of the book, we learned about the following:

- GPT-4o model – Deploying a GPT-4o model using Azure CLI

- Using DALL-E to generate images from text using Postman

- Converting speech to text using Whisper and PowerShell RAST

- Using GPT-4 Turbo and Vision to ask the model to describe images

I really hope you enjoyed this book and that it will form a solid foundation in your lifelong journey of learning and becoming an AI expert.

Index

D, E, F

W, X, Y, Z